Crimes Against Fecundity

RICHARD FALLIS, SERIES EDITOR

Crimes Against Fecundity

 Joyce and Population Control

Mary Lowe-Evans

Syracuse University Press

First Edition 1989
99 98 97 96 95 94 93 92 91 90 89   6 5 4 3 2 1

The excerpt from Patrick Kavanagh, "The Great Hunger," in *The Faber Book of Contemporary Irish Poetry* (London: Faber & Faber, 1986), is reprinted by permission of Mrs. Katherine Kavanagh and of Martin Brian & O'Keeffe Ltd, who published the poem in Kavanagh's *Collected Poems*, 1972.

The paper used in this publication meets the minimum requirements of American National Standard for Information Sciences—Permanence of Paper for Printed Library Materials, ANSI Z39.48-1984. ∞™

Library of Congress Cataloging-in-Publication Data

Lowe-Evans, Mary.
    Crimes against fecundity.

    (Irish studies)
    Bibliography: p.
    Includes index.
    1. Joyce, James, 1882–1941—Political and social
views. 2. Population policy in literature. 3. Birth
control in literature. 4. Emigration and immigration in
literature. 5. Fertility in literature. 6. Famines in
literature. 7. Ireland in literature. I. Title.
II. Series: Irish studies (Syracuse, N.Y.)
PR6019.09Z7165 1989   823'.912   88-35564
ISBN 0-8156-2460-3 (alk. paper)

MANUFACTURED IN THE UNITED STATES OF AMERICA

Thanks to Patrick McCarthy, Zack Bowen, Berni
and Shari Benstock, my children, and Sam. Also to Mildred Merrick
and Lynn McCorkle, librarians at the University of Miami.

Richard Fallis, Series Editor

Irish Studies presents a wide range of books interpreting important aspects of Irish life and culture to scholarly and general audiences. Irish literature is a special concern in the series, but works from the perspectives of the fine arts, history, and the social sciences are also welcome, as are studies which take multidisciplinary approaches.

Contents

MARY LOWE-EVANS is an Assistant Professor of English at the University of West Florida. She has contributed articles to *Studies in the Novel,* the *James Joyce Quarterly,* the *Journal of Modern Literature,* and the *Handbook of American Women's History.*

Conventions Adopted

All references are made to works listed among the "Works Cited" and are given parenthetically in the text. In most cases the source of the reference is identified in the text and the page number only is given in parentheses. Where the page number is not sufficient, the last name of the author precedes the page number. When there are two works by the same author listed in "Works Cited," the last name of the author, the title (or in some cases, a short title), and the page numbers are given.

References to Joyce's writings are abbreviated and cited parenthetically. In the case of *Ulysses*, both the Random House and the Gabler editions are cited. For the Random House edition, page and line numbers, separated by a period, are cited. The Random House citation is separated from the Gabler citation by a colon, and the Gabler edition is cited by chapter and line numbers, separated by a period. In the case of *Finnegans Wake*, page and line numbers, separated by a period, are cited. Standard editions and abbreviations used are as follows:

CW   *The Critical Writings of James Joyce*. Edited by Ellsworth Mason
        and Richard Ellmann. New York: Viking, 1959.
D   *"Dubliners": Text, Criticism, and Notes*. Edited by Robert
        Scholes and A. Walton Litz. New York: Viking, 1951.
E   *Exiles*. New York: Viking, 1968.
FW   *Finnegans Wake*. New York: Viking, 1939; 1967.
L 1, 2, 3 *Letters of James Joyce*. Vol. 1, edited by Stuart Gilbert. New
        York: Viking, 1957; reissued with corrections, 1965.
        Vols. 2 and 3, edited by Richard Ellmann. New York:
        Viking, 1966.

P   *"A Portrait of the Artist as a Young Man": Text, Criticism, and Notes.* Edited by Chester G. Anderson. New York: Viking, 1968.

SH   *Stephen Hero.* Edited by John J. Slocum and Herbert Cahoon. New York: New Directions, 1944, 1963.

U   *Ulysses.* New York: Random House, 1961.

and

Ulysses: A Critical and Synoptic Edition. Prepared by Hans Walter Gabler with Wolfhard Steppe and Claus Melchior. New York: Garland Publishing, 1984.

Crimes Against Fecundity

Introduction

In an attempt to clarify the meaning of "Oxen of the Sun," Joyce wrote to Frank Budgen that the idea underlying the episode is "the crime committed against fecundity by sterilizing the act of coition" (*L I*, 139). A close examination of the episode reveals, however, that the crime is impossibly complex, and in fact surfaces in a myriad of forms. Contraceptive devices, abortion, onanism, and permanent celibacy are the obvious subjects of discussion in the anteroom of the Holles Street Maternity Hospital. But constraining the frivolity of the party awaiting the arrival of the Purefoy baby is the ironic voice of the narrator, which seems itself to be the perpetrator of a far more pervasive and insidious crime. That crime involves the imposition of numerous, often conflicting, and transparent restrictions on the reproductive lives of individuals.

Joyce seems to have been acutely aware of the crimes Western civilization has committed against the physical, artistic, and spiritual fecundity of its citizens by attempting to modify their demographic behavior for ideological ends. These attempts take form, for example, in the rhetoric of a political economy that would justify the Famine of mid-nineteenth century Ireland as a way of reducing the surplus population and in the arguments of eugenicists who insist that the purity of the race requires close monitoring of those who would reproduce. The birth control movement of the first three decades of the twentieth century has contributed immeasurably to the population control debate. In Ireland, discussions of population control inevitably become associated with responses to the Famine, an event that has influenced patterns of and attitudes toward emigration, marriage, and celibacy ever since. These discussions are enmeshed in what Michel Foucault calls "the deployment of

1

sexuality," and have been given economic overtones by the various editions and interpretations of Thomas Robert Malthus's "Essay on Population."

This book exposes the influence of population control—in terms of the Famine, the Malthusian doctrine, the birth control movement, the Catholic church, and postwar populationism—on the Joyce canon, particularly "The Sisters," "Eveline," *A Portrait of the Artist as a Young Man*, "Oxen of the Sun," and *Finnegans Wake*. Population control was endlessly discussed during Joyce's lifetime, and in many important ways, Joyce's works were produced by that debate. By population control I mean pressures exerted so as to radically change the size or makeup of a given division of the population. Essential to my thesis is the belief that those pressures are most often rhetorical.

The specific subtopics of population control I consider here are Irish emigration from the Great Famine (ca. 1845–1851) through the early 1900s and the international birth control movement of the first three decades of this century. To reveal the affinity of these topics I chose the works of James Joyce, because they provide both a special sample and a typical case of the debate in progress. Special, because the rhetoric is concentrated, rich, and often conscious of the pressure that calls it into being; typical, because Joyce's works are unavoidably caught up in the currents of the discussion.

The Great Famine was a demographic and rhetorical benchmark in Irish history. The controversy surrounding the subject of emigration accumulated so much force during the Famine that the attitudes of the Irish are colored by it to this day. Marriage patterns and fertility rates altered so drastically in the years following the Famine that thrifty middle-aged bachelors and prolific, exhausted young mothers, existing side-by-side, had become stock characters on the Irish scene by the turn of the century. Evidence of the pressures created by the force of the Famine appear throughout Joyce's work, from Eveline's approach–avoidance conflict about leaving Ireland in *Dubliners* to the self-righteous celibacy of Shaun (as Jaun) in the *Wake*. The "paranoic bachelors and unfructified duennas" whom, among others, Mulligan blames "for any and every fall-ingoff in the calibre of the race" (*U* 418.41–42: *U* 14.1249–50) were caught in a frame of mind established during the Famine, while Mulligan himself seems to be influenced by eugenicist views current in turn-of-the-century Europe.

Dubliners and *Portrait* can be seen in the context of the continuing debate about Irish emigration. While nearly all critics, including Joyce himself, have considered Joyce a self-styled exile, my emphasis is on

Joyce as emigrant. As Richard Ellmann points out, Joyce was "neither bidden to leave nor forbidden to return" to Ireland (*James Joyce* 109); rather Joyce's work demonstrates that he was as susceptible to the pressures of the insistent cultural conversation about leaving Ireland as were emigrants with less linguistic sophistication. Joyce left Ireland in 1904 for the same reason that the vast majority of emigrants leave their homelands, because there is hope of greater economic security elsewhere. Joyce had heard of a position as English teacher for a Berlitz school on the Continent. If Joyce was an exile at all, he was an exile from Pola, then under Italian rule, along with all the other foreigners who were expelled in 1905. Still, to admit that he was an Irish emigrant would have been for Joyce comparable to admitting that he had been a student of the Christian Brothers—unacceptably déclassé. In transforming emigration into exile, Joyce was able to participate in a time-honored literary tradition wherein the young artist renounces everything, including his homeland, for the sake of his art. Joyce's expressed reasons for leaving, however, include his determination to live according to his moral nature. On close examination, that nature proves to be decidedly sexual; thus his reasons for leaving Ireland and his participation in the international movement toward sexual liberation become enmeshed.

I consider how the birth control movement entered the population debate in the Western world as a whole and the texts of "Oxen of the Sun" and *Finnegans Wake* in particular. That movement made sexual intercourse without the fear of pregnancy a public issue. Between 1876 and 1931, birth control became legitimate, respectable, and, to some extent, a civic duty. But the very freedom promised by the drive for conscious begetting quickly became conventionalized within a system of attitudes about sexuality and reproduction, a system which included racist and eugenicist attitudes and which was arguably as restrictive as the moral sanctions of religion have ever been. The various sexual liberties taken by Bloom, Molly's infidelity, and the recurring sexual indiscretions in the *Wake,* most of which are inconclusive and unsatisfying, incorporate conflicting values about reproduction and sexuality established in part by the birth control movement and its opponents. *Finnegans Wake* places the whole complex issue of population control on trial as real-life birth control advocates were placed on trial in the first decades of the century.

Throughout this work I reveal the impact of what Stephen Greenblatt might call "resonant texts" (5) on Joyce's works. Such texts range from histories of Ireland and the *Irish Homestead* to the newspaper reports of the obscenity trial of Margaret Sanger. The voices of two incalculably powerful authorities in the debate are invoked: the Roman

Catholic church and Thomas Robert Malthus. The Church has influenced attitudes on every aspect of life in Ireland, including emigration and birth control. Worldwide, it has insisted that birth control is a religious issue, the legitimacy of which must be determined by an institution appointed, like itself, by God. The proposals of Malthus challenged the Church's position, making population control an economic issue and bringing the subject of birth control into the public domain. Joyce's work responds to the ongoing conflict between these two powers. In many ways, however, the debate carried on by these two forces about controlling individual reproductive acts becomes absurd when carried out in the arenas of famine and world war. "Oxen" and the *Wake* reflect that irony.

I also invoke the philosophy of Michel Foucault. The original inspiration for this particular treatment of Joyce's works came from Foucault's observation that "one of the great innovations in techniques of power in the eighteenth century was the emergence of 'population' as an economic and political problem" (*History of Sexuality* 25). Like Foucault, I view the work of literature as the product of countless rhetorical pressures and currents. In this case those pressures are exerted on the sizes and qualities of populations. James Joyce does not disappear in the process of production, but rather becomes a particularly sensitive register of the intersecting currents. At various points throughout the text, I indicate how Foucault's theory of the deployment of sexuality—which argues that the nineteenth- and twentieth-century focus on sexuality is in fact a type of population control—is borne out both in Joyce's work and in the debate which helped produce it.

1

The Great Famine

"There is no cultural document that is not at the same time a record of barbarism"
—Walter Benjamin, "Edward Fuchs, Collector and Historian" 359.

The idea that population can and must be manipulated became fixed in the mind of Western civilization with the dissemination of Thomas Malthus's first "Essay on Population," which was published in 1798 (see "Population Ethics" 1234). The two postulates set forth by Malthus in the opening pages of that essay have informed our thinking on population control ever since. Malthus proposed "that food is necessary to the existence of man [and], that the passion between the sexes is necessary and will remain nearly in its present state" (Malthus 8). From these two apparently innocent pronouncements derives a plethora of arguments, pro and con, about the need to control human fertility vis-à-vis the availability of resources. The debate continues even to this day, albeit in widely divergent and strangely hybrid forms. Frequently, discourse has been transformed into policy, and policy into action (or inaction) as the need arises.

Ironically, population control gained acceptance as a doctrine during the nineteenth century simultaneously with the notion that for the best economic results, government must leave the people alone. Laissez-faire philosophy, ostensibly encouraging individual freedom, thus diverted attention from the fact that population had come under relentless scrutiny and pressure from a myriad of sources at a number of points: birth and death rates, marriage patterns, genetic characteristics, and mi-

5

gratory habits. "At the heart of this economic and political problem of population," Michel Foucault contends, "was sex" (*History of Sexuality* 25). The result of these innumerable pressures on sexuality is that the population of the Western world has been moving toward some as yet inscrutable norm of reproductive behavior.

Sex, food, individuality, and control of life forces are important themes in Joyce's works largely because he was caught up in the arguments about population; in many ways his works have been rewritten, displaced, diminished, or enlarged by these arguments. Examined closely against the background of Joyce's life and times, each work is discovered to be pointing to some real event or events, some other text or texts, some larger discourse involving the manipulation of vital forces. For example, "A Painful Case" is an interpretation of an actual event in the life of Joyce's brother, Stanislaus, who subsequently created a text about the event in his diary (Ellmann, *James Joyce* 133). Joyce thereafter appropriated and interpreted that text in such a way that Mr. Duffy, the central character, became "the type of the male celibate" (*S. Joyce* 174).

Some time after the Great Famine in the mid-nineteenth century, the high incidence of permanent male celibacy in Ireland had become implicated in the case of the diminishing population and had thus been established as a part of the discourse on that problem (see Kennedy 139–72). Furthermore, in texts on sexology and eugenics such as those of Havelock Ellis (which Joyce knew), celibacy had become both a symptom and a cause of various eccentricities leading to physical and emotional sterility like Mr. Duffy's. It might be argued, then, that the real event, the record of that event, and the discussions about population and sexology all function as authors of "A Painful Case." Or, put another way, all contribute to the author-function of that text. Each contributor has registered its influence on Joyce, who has consequently given it a hearing (or reading) in his work. In "What Is An Author?" Foucault defines the author-function as just such a "plurality of self" as I have argued to be the producer of "A Painful Case."

According to the Foucauldian definition, it would seem that the discourse whose topic is imposed most persistently and ingeniously into what Foucault calls the "universe of discourses" is likely to contribute most significantly to the author-function. Furthermore, it is clear that the author-function may be effectively served by a momentous historical event, particularly one that is readily incorporated into the current dominant discourse.

Some events naturally contribute more potently to the author-function than others because of their impact on all aspects of the being—biological, psychological, political, economic, moral. The American Civil War, for example, has inspired a far more influential and complicated discourse than the creation of the Colorado Territory, which took place at about the same time. In a sense, the American Civil War helped to author the Faulkner canon. Similarly, the Great Famine, which began in Ireland in 1845 or 1846, contributes to the authorship of Joyce's works. The Famine established a certain mode of thinking, writing, and speaking in Ireland—a rhetoric and a set of attitudes distinguishable from anything previous—because it uniquely combined natural and economic methods of population control. Even today, the Famine affects the responses of the Irish to population control.

In a study based not only on extensive research into documents produced during and immediately after the Famine, but also on current accounts of its effects, Thomas Gallagher concludes that the Famine was "not a separate or isolated part of Irish history but, rather, the nadir of that history, so stark and devastating in its effects . . . that it was to shape the attitudes of the Irish all over the world on into the twentieth century" (*xiv*). In 1888, Phillipe Daryl, in *Ireland's Disease*, said of Ireland and the Famine, "never did she rise from it" (178); writing in that same year, the Honourable Emily Lawless found that "between the Ireland of the past and the Ireland of the present the Famine lies like a black stream, all but blotting out and effacing the past" (401).

Following Queen Victoria's ill-timed visit to Ireland in 1900, Percy French, the popular singer and entertainer, "wrote a witty account of an imaginary after-dinner speech made by the queen" (O'Connor 270). That speech includes the lines,

> "An' all that gammon," sez she
> "About me bringin' the famine," sez she
> "Now Maud'll write," sez she
> "That I brought the blight" sez she
> "Or altered the saysons" sez she
> "For political raysons," sez she

Joyce was eighteen and very much in tune with popular culture when this bit of satire made the rounds; and four years later, a pivotal year in the life of Joyce and in the many reform movements taking place in Ireland, the Famine was still on the mind of the Irish nation. Both Sir Horace Plunkett and Michael Davitt, whose radically different histories of Ireland were published in 1904, attributed to the Famine tremendous power over the spirit and behavior of the Irish people (see Plunkett 14; Davitt 47–65).

Joyce had Davitt's book with him in Trieste, and in *Joyce's Politics,* Dominic Manganiello suggests that Davitt may have provided Joyce with a background for his "anarchist attack upon ecclesiastical and imperial powers when he places responsibility for the Great Famine on the 'political and spiritual governors of the people' " (84). Mr. Deasy remembers the Famine: "I saw three generations since O'Connell's time. I remember the famine" (*U* 31.18–19: *U* 2.269). Joyce recalls it in "Ireland, Island of Saints and Sages" (*CW* 172), and in "Cyclops," the Citizen provides a résumé of its consequences:

> We have our greater Ireland beyond the sea. They were driven out of house and home in the black 47. Their mudcabins and their shielings were laid low by the batteringram and the *Times* rubbed its hands and told the whitelivered Saxons there would soon be as few Irish in Ireland as redskins in America. Even the grand Turk sent us his piastres. But the Sassenach tried to starve the nation at home while the land was full of crops that the British hyenas bought and sold in Rio de Janeiro. Ay, they drove out the peasants in hordes. Twenty thousand of them died in the coffinships. But those that came to the land of the free remember the land of bondage. And they will come again and with a vengeance, no cravens, the sons of Granuaile, the champions of Kathleen ni Houlihan. (*U* 329.36– 330.8: *U* 12.1364–75)

The *Times* commentary actually read "Soon a Celt will be as rare on the banks of the Liffey as a red man on the Manhattan" (quoted in Gallagher 143); thus the Citizen's account of the Famine's aftermath is as substantially accurate as more official versions. Even the prophecy, implicit in the Citizen's tirade, that vengeance would come from America, was already being fulfilled: the avowedly violent Fenian movement, begun during the 1860s, was begun by Irishmen who had emigrated there during the Famine (Averill 12). Although the specific references to the Famine in his works demonstrate Joyce's thorough familiarity with its circumstances, it is in his rhetoric, his attitudes toward his subjects, and his complicated response to the pressures of population control that the Famine intrudes most forcefully into his writing.

Two demographic characteristics that recur in Joyce's works and are considered typical of Ireland—postponed marriages and permanent celibacy—first became evident after the Great Famine. In *The Irish: Emigration, Marriage, and Fertility,* Robert E. Kennedy reports that for several decades prior to the Famine Ireland did not have unusually high rates in either of these categories, but after 1851 (the year of the first post–Famine census) there was a sudden rise. "Obviously, a great change occurred between 1841 and 1851 in the proportion of Irish persons willing to postpone marriage, a change associated with events surrounding the 1845–48 famine" (142). Although Kennedy does not argue for the continuing effects of the Famine *per se* on marriage patterns in Ireland, his study shows that the Famine initially influenced them.

Kennedy provides strong evidence, too, that as a result of the Famine, the Irish began to take their economic plight more seriously than ever before and to respond to it at every level of activity. Underlying those responses was a perception, inculcated by the British, that the Famine was a Malthusian reproach, a "lesson about the tragedy of a population outstripping its means of existence" (Ross 196). Kennedy therefore argues that the patterns of late marriage and celibacy have been maintained in Ireland, not for religious reasons, as many believe, but for economic ones. As a way of improving and maintaining one's standard of living, postponed marriage or celibacy was often chosen as an alternative to emigration. On the other hand, the high birthrate among married couples is typically attributed to the sanctions against birth control imposed by the Catholic church and enforced (until very recently) by the government.

Bob Doran, the thirty-four-year-old "celibate" in "The Boarding House," provides an interesting illustration of Kennedy's thesis. Although Doran has good qualifications for marriage—a steady job, a savings account, and a depleted supply of wild oats—his instinct "urged him to remain free, not to marry. Once you are married you are done for, it said" (*D* 66). Lenehan and Gallaher also illustrate Kennedy's findings. Lenehan "might yet be able to settle down ... if he could only come across some good simple-minded girl with a little of the ready" (*D* 58), and Gallaher is determined "to marry money. She'll have a good fat account at the bank or she won't do for me" (*D* 81).

Helene Cixous recognizes in Joyce's works a persistent "satire against bachelors" exposing characters as various and yet similar as Robert Hand, Blazes Boylan, Buck Mulligan, and Shaun, men who share a "defensive egoism," who want to "enjoy life without paying the price," and who "completely lack humanity" (96). Bob Doran is such a bachelor who has let his defenses down. In creating these characters, Joyce was responding to a phenomenon in Irish society that was perceived to be, and in some ways actually was, a result of the Famine.

Writing several decades after Joyce, Patrick Kavanagh directly expresses the link between the Famine and the permanent celibate in his long narrative poem, "The Great Hunger." In that poem, Paddy McGuire, enslaved by the land and his duty to his mother:

> ———stayed with his mother til she died
> At the age of ninety-one.
> She stayed too long,
> Wife and mother in one
> When she died
> The knuckle-bones were cutting the skin of her son's backside
> And he was sixty-five. (30)

Kavanagh's collected poems first appeared in 1964, two years after the publication of Cecil Woodham-Smith's extensive study of the Famine, also entitled *The Great Hunger.* Clearly, the Famine had left an ineradicable mark on Irish sensibilities.

Why did the Great Famine have such deep, wide, and long effects? Ireland had, after all, suffered many previous famines. But the Famine of the mid-nineteenth century was different, extending farther, lasting longer, killing or banishing more people, and being better documented than any other. Most horrifying of all, moreover, was the realization that its causes were in large measure artificial. The Famine of 1845–1851 was allowed to happen in order to carry out currently accepted laws of population which had become givens in Western economic philosophy. The Irish people were consequently subjected to a devastating and humiliating communal experience to comply with the tenets of a doctrine that relegated human beings to economic functions. According to Woodham-Smith, "the influence of *laissez-faire* on the treatment of Ireland during the famine is impossible to exaggerate. . . . the behaviour of the British authorities only becomes explicable when their fanatical belief in private enterprise [is] borne in mind" (54). It is the combination of the physically debilitating nature of the Famine and its ideological justification that has produced a complex, rich, and powerful discourse which seems always to influence discussions of population control in Ireland.

Descriptions of the arrival of the Famine are striking. "A peculiarly dense white fog ... was believed by all who were in Ireland at the time to have carried the blight with it in its folds" (Lawless 396); "a terrible sense of danger and dread descended on the land like the thick fog that covered the countryside on the fatal night, the fog that people in Ireland still speak of as 'the potato fog' " (Gallagher 8); "an extremely white vapour resembling a snowstorm appeared" (O'Rourke 15). The sight of the fog was soon followed by the stench of rotting plants, "a sulphurous, sewerlike smell carried by the wind. . . . the odour from decaying flesh could not have been more offensive" (quoted in Gallagher 4, 6).

The opening lines of book 1, chapter 3 of *Finnegans Wake* may owe something to such descriptions of the Famine's onset: "Chest Cee! 'Sdense! Corpo di barragio! you spoof of visibility in a freakfog. . . . Therewith was released in that kingsrick of Humidia a poisoning volume of cloud barrage indeed" (*FW* 48.1–5). Since this chapter of the *Wake* introduces the confusion of the modern, civil age and the contradictions and inequities involved in democratic and capitalistic forms of government, it is appropriate that it open with a reference to a national catastrophe that eventually became justified by capitalistic rhetoric. Near the end of the chapter, Earwicker sits, apparently at stool, "behind faminebuilt walls, [mourning] the flight of his wild guineese" (*FW* 71.2–4). Clearly, the Famine and its resulting emigration remain very much a part of the modern Irish memory that Earwicker here represents.

The number of people who actually starved to death in the Famine is reckoned at 729,033 (Paul-Dubois 72). With limited relief offered by soup kitchens and Indian meal, the emaciated victims were left to eat whatever was available, including rats and docile dogs, while, ironically, other ravenous dogs ate the flesh of unburied dead bodies. The Stephen Dedalus who muses about dogs and bones and grandmothers' bodies shares a collective memory in which exists a communal revulsion to the Famine. In *Portrait*, Stephen, the city boy, is brought closer to that unconscious memory by Davin, the young peasant who "worshipped the sorrowful legend of Ireland" (*P* 181). One of the greatest sorrows recounted in that legend is the Famine. In "Lestrygonians," Bloom, too, thinks of emaciated victims, "hot fresh blood they prescribe for decline. Blood always needed. Insidious. Lick it up, smoking hot, thick sugary. Famished ghosts. Ah, I'm hungry" (*U* 171.16–19: *U* 8.729–31). Bloom's vision of famished ghosts might well be imagined progeny of the Famine.

In addition to those who starved to death, 1,180,409 emigrants left Ireland between 1846 and 1851, and 17 per cent of them died on the journey to their promised land (O'Rourke 499). These were the forefathers of the "missing twenty millions of Irish [who] should be here today" of whom the Citizen speaks (*U* 326.11–12: *U* 12.1240–41). To the emigration figures must also be added the countless numbers who died of typhus, the symptoms of which include "rigor ... [and a] clouded mental state that many at first mistakenly associated with drunkenness, then muscular twitchings, the delirium, and finally the deep stupor caused by leakage of blood vessels that fed oxygen to the brain ... near the end the skin took on a dusky hue" (Gallagher 61).

On December 20, 1846, the Cork *Examiner* ran an editorial giving a lengthy description of a typical Famine scene. The terminology used to describe the prevailing conditions would be frequently repeated in all varieties of literature about Ireland for decades after the Famine had ended and would, to some extent, ensure that some of those conditions continued to prevail:

> A terrible apathy hangs over the poor of Skibbereen; starvation has destroyed every generous sympathy; despair has made them hardened and insensible, and they sullenly await their doom with indifference and without fear. Death is in every hovel; disease and famine, its dread precursors, have fastened the young and old, the strong and feeble, the mother and the infant; whole families lie together on the damp floor devoured by fever, without a human being to wet their burning lips or raise their languid heads; the husband dies by the side of the wife, and she knows not that he is beyond the reach of earthly suffering; the same rag covers the festering remains of mortality and the skeleton forms of the living, who are unconscious of the horrible contiguity; rats devour the corpse, and there is no energy among the living to scare them from their horrid banquet. ... Without food or fuel, bed or bedding, whole families are shut up in naked hovels, dropping one by one into the arms of death.

George Henry Moore, father of the novelist, was so horrified by scenes of devastation like this one that he decided to enter politics in order to improve the lot of the Mayo peasants. He became so extreme in his views that, after one particularly heated speech against the government, the *Times* called for his arrest (O'Connor 55).

Mention of the rats at "their horrid banquet" in the above account recalls the "obese grey rat" that first appears in "Hades" and resurfaces in several subsequent episodes. In *Ulysses* the rat serves to constantly undercut the impression of relative prosperity in the Dublin of 1904. Bloom thinks "one of those chaps would make short work of a fellow. Pick the bones clean no matter who he was" (*U* 114.21–22: *U* 6.980–81). Indeed the Famine, like Bloom's rat, had a decidedly levelling effect on the population of Ireland, destroying families from within and without regardless of social class. And like that rat, the Famine surfaced again and again (albeit rhetorically) in the Dublin of 1904.

In addition to the physical degradation described above, the Irish were visited by epidemics of severe dysentery and scurvy (both complications of starvation) and cholera. An epidemic of cholera that hit Dublin in 1849 in the wake of the Famine only exacerbated the city's still festering wounds. "The cholera plague spread rapidly, and the city hospitals were soon crowded out, temporary sheds being erected at Kilmainham for the accommodation of sufferers" (Sheridan 122). During that cholera epidemic (which incidentally took the life of the early nineteenth-century Irish poet James Clarence Mangan [Sheridan 122]), and while the Famine raged on, John Stanislaus Joyce was born in Cork, where the blight had begun, the most popular port of exit for the emigrants, and the site of one of the famous soup kitchens. Inveterate storyteller that he was, John Joyce must surely have recounted to young James (perhaps on the trip to dispose of the Cork properties in 1894) some of the gruesome Famine lore surviving from Cork in particular and Ireland in general.

An example of such lore is the poem "The Famine Year," written by Speranza (Oscar Wilde's mother), and according to Ulick O'Connor (100), recited around firesides throughout the country:

> Weary men, what reap ye?—"Golden corn for the stranger."
> What sow ye?—"Human corses that await for the Avenger."
> Fainting forms, all hunger-stricken, what see you in the offing?
> "Stately ships to bear our food away amid the stranger's scoffing."
> There's a proud array of soldiers—what do they round your door?
> "They guard our masters granaries from the thin hands of the
>   poor."

In his own "first true work" of literature (as he called *A Brilliant Career*), Joyce, too, chose to depict the devastating effects of a plague. William Archer called this (now lost) play of Joyce's "a huge fable of politics and pestilence" (quoted in Ellmann 78, 79). But the Famine and the plagues it engendered were no fables, as Joyce knew. Furthermore, the Famine was largely the product of the rhetorical machinations of politicians, another fact of which Joyce was aware, as the Citizen's account makes clear.

The Sunday constitutionals that Stephen Dedalus took with his father and granduncle involved "trudging along the road or standing in some grimy wayside publichouse [as] his elders spoke constantly of the subjects [near] their hearts, of Irish politics, of Munster and the legends of their own family, to all of which Stephen lent an avid ear" (*P* 62). Gallagher's study shows that virtually every Irish family history has its own Famine episode, and the legends evolving from these episodes have created an important oral tradition. In 1955 a compilation of accounts given by Irish men and women old enough to remember their parents' stories of the Famine was made. It is now housed in the Irish Folklore Department, University College, Dublin.

Liam O'Flaherty drew on the oral tradition for his critically acclaimed novel, *Famine*, published in 1937. "As for the Great Famine, O'Flaherty knew it through the vast body of folklore surrounding it" (Cahalan 140). In "Proteus," as Stephen walks slowly along the strand, conjuring up his ancestors, he seems to draw on the same tradition when he thinks of "Famine, plague and slaughters. Their blood is in me, their lusts my waves" (*U* 45.17–18: *U* 3.306–7).

Aside from the political and psychological implications of the Famine, it should be increasingly obvious that the very real physical consequences—the humiliating distortions and decay of the body and its functions, leading to ignominious death—initiated a distinctively corporeal rhetoric. Postures of "apathy," "sullen despair," and "indifference," as well as activities such as "bloodletting," and states of "rigor," come up again and again in Famine commentaries. Synonyms and modifications of these terms, such as "paralysis," "misery," "stupor," and "anaemia," also hammer home the rhetoric of corporeal misery. All represent varying degrees of suffering and death; all suggest a living hell. Certainly the Great Famine was an unprecedented assault on the senses even in the annals of Ireland, a nightmare of history from which there was no escape since the rhetoric it engendered would not let it die. "No tongue can describe, no understanding can conceive the misery and wretchedness," declared Father Matthew (the famous whiskey-abstinence priest from Cork), providing an ironic twist to Saint Paul's attempt to describe heaven (O'Rourke 410). But descriptions of the Famine proliferated with new vigor at the turn of the century.

As soon as the people grasped the reality of the hell to which Ireland had been reduced, those who were healthy enough determined to escape. A statistical study of the resulting situation concludes that "the nineteenth century demographic history of Ireland falls naturally into two periods: that preceding and that following the Great Famine of

1846–51. Before that catastrophe population growth was extremely rapid" (Cousens 387). Gallagher's more emotionally charged account relates that "with the worst famine in recorded history . . . thousands saw emigration as the only remedy. No longer was it a question of whether to go, but of when and how to leave" (Gallagher 118). Irish emigration has ever since been linked with Famine modes of thinking, speaking, and writing.

Daryl and Lawless each made the connection in their 1888 histories, Plunkett and Davitt both suggested the relationship in 1904, and in 1907 Joyce declared that "even today, the flight of the wild geese continues. Every year, Ireland, decimated as she already is, loses 60,000 of her sons. From 1850 to the present day, more than 5,000,000 emigrants have left for America, and . . . the poor anaemic, almost lifeless body [of Ireland] lies in agony, the rulers give orders and the priests administer last rites" ("Ireland, Island of Saints," *CW* 172). In his introduction to L. Paul-DuBois's *Contemporary Ireland* (1908), Thomas Kettle urged the Irish citizen to "come free of the egoism and pessimism which have remained in his blood since the Great Famine" (*x*). In 1953 John A. O'Brien and his contributors continued to insist on the Famine–emigration link in *The Vanishing Irish*. And in 1968, R. C. Geary, writing on "Present Day and Future Emigration from Ireland in Historical Perspective," gave as a reason for the "strong" public feeling against emigration "the folk memory. In the Irish mind emigration is indelibly associated with the Famine, the greatest catastrophe afflicting a people until Hitler. I recall a speaker . . . saying (I thought with some truth) 'The Irish are the only people who regard emigration as tragic' " (Geary 4).

In the following chapter, I will discuss the link between Joyce's life and works and Famine–emigration rhetoric. Meanwhile, it is important to examine the psychological and economic effects of the Famine, inextricably bound up as they are with the physical ones. The immediate urge of the Irish people to escape the consequences of an overwhelming natural disaster requires no explanation. What is more difficult to understand is the ongoing effect of the Great Famine on Irish population trends and attitudes. Kettle classified these attitudes as egoism and pessimism; they might also be characterized as self-justification and self-loathing.

At the outbreak of the blight no one thought of accusing England of causing the potato rot, but as the Famine spread and official relief was not forthcoming, it became clear that England had adopted a laissez faire attitude. The government blamed the Famine for reducing the "surplus" population of Ireland, an effect the English government had desired in the first place. The Malthusian doctrine thus invoked, England began to employ a form of what Foucault calls "bio-power ... an indispensable element in the development of capitalism [which was not] possible without the controlled insertion of bodies into the machinery of production and the adjustment of the phenomena of population to economic processes [capitalism] needed the growth of both these factors, their reinforcement ... and *docility*" (*History of Sexuality* 140–41, emphasis mine).

The Famine provided England with a convenient means of adjusting the population of Ireland—a plot it had been attempting to carry out since at least 1829, when its "clearance" policies began to be vigorously enforced—and blaming that adjustment on Providence. The "docility" of the people was guaranteed by their indebtedness to their landlords, their colonial status, and most immediately, by their starving condition. It is this perceived docility, I propose, that is the key to the enigmatic attitude toward population control that the Famine created in all of the Irish, including Joyce.

The most salient feature of the Famine, and the one which placed it in the category of Foucault's bio-power, was its artificiality. Although the potato crop had failed, it was not the only crop in Ireland; rather, it was the only crop that could sustain the Irish year after year given the minimal amount of land allotted for their own use. The remainder of the land was dedicated to crops used to pay English landlords. Those crops remained healthy during the Famine. "It was not want of foodstuffs that caused the famine. But the produce of the land was used up in paying the landlords' rent. There was famine in the midst of plenty" (Paul-Dubois 73), This was undoubtedly the same race of landlords to whom Swift made his modest proposal in 1729.

Interestingly, as Eric B. Ross pointed out in 1981, during the Famine "the English Prime Minister, John Russell, and his Foreign Minister, Lord Palmerston—as well as other members of his cabinet—were themselves absentee landlords" (199). One of Ross's theses is that the Malthusian ideology promulgated by England during and after the Famine turned the potato into a scapegoat: "The potato, an essential element of the English system in Ireland, thus was used as a convenient scapegoat by the beneficiaries of the very system that had encouraged its increasing prominence" (203).

The potato, once suggestive only of fertility, thus became a contradictory symbol in Ireland. The contradictions implicit in the symbology of the potato are particularly exploited in "Circe." In the pocket of Leopold Bloom, who is "being made a scapegoat of" (*U* 457.9: *U* 15.775), the

potato is a complex talisman combining his poor Irish "mamma's pana-
cea" for rheumatism with a symbol of Irish national tragedy (*U* 435.27:
U 15.202). When the "daughters of Erin" in parodic litany ask that the
"potato Preservative against Plague and Pestilence, pray for us" (*U*
499.3: *U* 15.9), they invoke the potato both as communal life saver and
preventer (preservative). And, on the breast of Old Gummy Granny,
"the deathflower of the potato blight" (*U* 595.5–7: *U* 15.4579–80) is
equally complex. Gummy Granny and her potato blossom corsage com-
bine embittered fanaticism with impotence, as "poor old Ireland" had
done in the face of the Famine.

Added to the insult of feeding the English while its own people
starved was the injury to Ireland of the "clearances" mentioned earlier.
Beginning about 1829, when tillage had ceased to pay the absentee landlords (who comprised about 70 percent of the total number) as well as
they would have liked, the English had inaugurated a campaign calling
for the expulsion of the smaller peasants from the land, the razing of
their houses, and the conversion of agricultural lands into pasture. Ireland was thereby transformed from granary to stockyard and dairy for
Great Britain. During the Famine, the clearances continued unchecked,
and even increased. Peasants, desperate to keep at least a roof over their
heads, dared not touch the produce "marked" by the landlords for rent.
That produce—enough cattle, wheat, oats, and barley to feed twice the
population of Ireland—was used to maintain the economic and physical
health of England. Speranza's account of "The Famine Year" comes to
mind.

Responses to the plight of the Irish ran the gamut from sympathy
to scorn. Philanthropic and religious groups in America, the British col-
onies, and even England sent help. But the official British response was
largely judgmental, and profoundly economic. In 1847, Sir Charles
Trevelyan declared in Parliament that "being altogether beyond the
power of man, the cure [for the Irish Question and overpopulation] had
been applied by the direct stroke of an all-wise Providence in a manner
as unexpected and as unthought of as it is likely to be effectual." Based
on the comments of Trevelyan and other public officials, Gallagher concludes that "in the eyes of most of the members of Parliament, England
was exonerated ... because all agreed that there must be no interference
with the natural course of trade" (86–87).

Michael Davitt, whose family had been evicted from their cottage
in County Mayo in 1851 (O'Connor 33), gives one of the most scathing of
all of the turn-of-the-century accounts of the Famine. Davitt quotes a
Catholic bishop speaking from his pulpit in New York at this time:

"They call it God's famine.... No! God's famine is known by the general scarcity of food which is its consequence. There is no general scarcity.... But political economy, finding Ireland too poor to buy the produce of its own labor, exported that harvest to a better market, and left the people to die of famine or live by alms" (51). What money the government did provide for the relief of Ireland was either tied up in so much official red tape that little of it benefitted the people or was designated for the building of useless roads which led nowhere.

International censure began to force England to share some of the responsibility for the starving Irish, and it soon became clear that an effective way for England to relieve its conscience publicly and at the same time cooperate in the handiwork of the Famine was to provide assistance for the emigrants. As one Irishman put it, the landlords discovered "that the best plan would be to get completely rid of those who were so heavy a burden upon them ... at the same time publishing to the world, as an act of brotherly love and kindness, a deal of crafty, calculating selfishness" (Gallagher 143). Financially assisted emigration thus became both penance and absolution for England and tainted the purity of intention of those leaving Ireland.

Another recompense made by the British was the establishment of soup kitchens, the most notorious of which was erected in Dublin.

> Perhaps nothing during the famine years more appropriately symbolized England's "helping hand" to Ireland than Soyer's Dublin soup kitchen, for it was there on April 5, 1847, with the beating of drums and the sounding of horns, with the Union Jack proudly flying from the kitchen's smoking chimney and a splendidly attired gentry nodding its approval, that the British government fed the Irish a soup incapable of keeping a newborn cat alive. (Gallagher 99–100)

In "Lestrygonians," after noticing the title *Why I Left The Church of Rome* on display in Thomas Connellan's bookstore, Bloom recalls hearing that "they used to give pauper children soup to change to protestants in the time of the potato blight. Society over the way papa went to for the conversion of poor jews. Same bait" (*U* 180.27–30: *U* 8.1071–74). Bloom's idea of a communal kitchen mentioned earlier in the episode has its analogue in Irish history in Soyer's Dublin soup kitchen. "Suppose that communal kitchen years to come perhaps. All trotting down with porringers and tommycans to be filled. Devour contents in the street.... After you with our incorporated drinking cup. ... Rub off the microbes with your handkerchief. Next chap rubs on a new batch with his. ... Want a soup pot as big as the Phoenix Park" (*U* 170.27–41: *U* 8.704–15).

Soyer's Dublin soup kitchen, which housed a "three hundred gallon steam boiler," was a wood-framed canvas building located near the main entrance to Phoenix Park. At the sound of a bell, one hundred of the destitute entered and, using chained soupspoons, consumed what was euphemistically called "The Poor Man's Regenerator." As soon as the bowls and spoons had been swabbed and the bowls refilled, another hundred starving Irish men, women, and children were ushered in. Each cycle took six minutes; a thousand people were fed every hour (Gallagher 95–97). After making a chemical analysis of the soup, the English medical journal *The Lancet* pronounced it worthless: "This soup quackery (for it is no less) seems to be taken by the rich as a salve for their consciences" (quoted in Gallagher 98).

In the meantime, the conscience of Ireland, which sixty-odd years later Joyce insisted had yet to be created, was being sorely tried. Questions originally raised by the Famine about the moral fiber of the people were being pressed more urgently than ever as Joyce left Ireland in 1904, when renaissance and reform were the order of the day. The questions, all more or less directly related to the issue of population control, sprang from perceptions about how the Irish people had handled themselves during the crisis of starvation.

Aside from the general mental stupor brought on by inanition and disease, shocking cases of cannibalism had been reported, and families had been deserted by one or both parents. Not only had the fertility rate declined, but the very instinct for sex had diminished drastically (see Gallagher). Most problematic in these various reductions of the life force was the mirroring of the biological impotence of the Irish in their apparent powerlessness to stop the English landlords from driving them off the land and shipping out crops which could have saved their lives. The 1851 Census of Ireland emphasizes the docility and passivity of the people in the face of this crisis: "Through [the Famine] the forebearance of the Irish peasantry, and the calm submission with which they bore the deadliest ills that can fall on man can scarcely be paralleled in the annals of any people" (quoted in Gallagher 71).

Michael Davitt opens his chapter on "The Great Famine" with a forceful castigation of Irish docility. Important to our future discussion of Joyce's work is the shift of blame for the Famine that occurs in Davitt's history: the blame has expanded to include the Catholic church. Joyce owned Davitt's history and evidence of the influence of the Famine chapter appears in several places in Joyce's works. (I will discuss that evidence at greater length in this and the following chapters.) Davitt is particularly harsh on Ireland's Church-induced "perverted morality":

> It is related that Mr. John O'Connell, M.P., eldest son of the Liberator, read aloud in Conciliation Hall, Dublin, a letter he had received from a Catholic Bishop in West Cork, in 1847, in which this sentence occurred, "The famine is spreading with fearful rapidity, and scores of persons are dying of starvation and fever, but the tenants are bravely paying their rents." Whereupon John O'Connell exclaimed, in proud tones, "I thank God I live among a people who would rather die of hunger than defraud their landlords of the rent!" It is not, unfortunately, on record that the author of this atrocious sentiment was forthwith kicked from the hall into the sink of the Liffey. He was not even hissed by his audience; so dead to every sense and right of manhood were the Irish people reduced in those years of hopeless life and of a fetid pestilence of perverted morality. (47)

The "perverted morality," like the defective conscience, of the Irish was widely asserted by Davitt and others in the early twentieth century; in fact the phrases are synonymous. The case for that perversion, as Davitt's remarks demonstrate, invoked the Famine for justification. Five years before he left Ireland for good, Joyce began establishing his own brief against the conscience of Ireland, and in it the Famine once more figures.

In May 1899, still undecided about leaving the country, Joyce was enlisted in a "splendid quarrel," the very terms of which would provide justification for emigrating (Ellmann, *James Joyce* 66). The subject of controversy was Yeats's *The Countess Cathleen,* the much-heralded opening play of the Irish Literary Theater, to which the public response demonstrates the complex workings of the Famine on Irish sensibilities. Nearly all of the controversial issues raised by the Famine are handled in the play, in which Yeats's countess sells her soul to merchants—actually agents of the devil—in order to save her country from a devastating famine. The peasants' only hope for survival is "to rob or starve" (13). The "lies that [the peasant woman] had heard in chapel" have caused her to be unduly scrupulous (24). A merciless god has poured nothing "out of his bag but famine" (10). And the merchants, analogous to the political economy of the British, "buy and sell" human souls (9).

Joyce attended the premiere of *The Countess Cathleen*, which Cardinal Logue, without having read it, pronounced heretical. While many of Joyce's friends in the audience booed and hissed what they felt to be the play's unpatriotic or heretical passages, Joyce "clapped vigorously" (Ellmann, *James Joyce* 67). Joyce refused to join his friends Thomas Kettle, Francis Skeffington, John Francis Byrne, and Richard Sheehy in signing a letter protesting the play's "travesties of the Irish Catholic Celt." Ellmann suggests that what appealed to Joyce in the play was "the theme of a Faustlike scapegoat for the race" (Ellmann, *James Joyce* 66, 67). At least as impressive to Joyce must have been Yeats's choice of subject—a great famine and its revelations about the Irish character. Yeats's play was in many ways as incriminating an indictment of the religion of the Irish peasant as Michael Davitt's straightforward condemnation of moral perversion quoted above, and Yeats, like Davitt, cited the Famine as his authority.

While those who argued for the perverted morality of the Irish presented the Famine as a prime example from the past, they would point to apathetic political responses, sexual inhibitions and aberrations, and continuing emigration as contemporary evidence of the Famine's consequences. The Church had become implicated in the case in a variety of ways, the most damning of which Davitt identifies in his chapter on the Famine: it had been assigned responsibility for the docility of the people. In his fiction, George Moore represents variations on the moral perversion theme, and in *Stephen Hero* through the *Wake*, Joyce provides still others.

The hypothesis upon which these themes are based might be stated as follows: The Church had inculcated a scrupulousness of conscience into Irish thinking that devalued secular life and individuality. This scrupulousness manifested itself in the forms of docility, passivity, apathy, and submissiveness to the Church, the most glaring example of which was the national response to the Great Famine. Furthermore, the Church's continuing "scrupulous meanness," especially with regard to sexual matters, meant (a) insisting too strenuously upon celibacy in young people, (b) forcing large families on married couples who could not afford them, and (c) driving the most vigorous of the population out of the country because of its moral stance and its denial of the individual's right to control his or her own body.

Thus, the exploratory discourse about Ireland's population problem that was dominant during and immediately following the Great Famine, when the causes were perceived to be natural and/or politico-economic, came to include a polemic about the Church's stand on sexuality. Concerns about starvation and emigration became concerns about sexual deprivation and emigration. Much of the vocabulary of the Famine, which had derived from the taxonomy of starvation and disease, was retained and integrated with sexual terminology. What Foucauldians now call "the deployment of sexuality" was well under way.

The transition paralleled the development of the nineteenth-century discourse on population in general, a debate which almost imperceptibly moved from an emphasis on the vital activities of whole populations to the sexual activities of the individuals within the whole. The growing fields of genetics, eugenics, sexology, and psychology enriched the lexicon and increased the strength of the discourse. The birth control movement made an incalculable contribution to the debate. Countering the force of these apparently liberating movements, however, was a reemphasis on populationism and family stability, especially in Europe, during the interwar years. Ireland was slowly influenced by these larger movements, but it also retained a unique voice, thanks in part to the Great Famine.

There can be no doubt that Joyce was surrounded by and immersed in complex Famine rhetoric and the debate about the Church's responsibility for the perverted conscience of Ireland. For example, in Stephen Gwynn's *Today and Tomorrow in Ireland,* a book that Joyce reviewed in 1903, Gwynn remarks that "whoever wishes to serve Ireland will have no easy task. . . . Her lassitude is the lassitude of anaemia; she has been drained for so long, that she is . . . *saignée à blanc*" (xviii). Elsewhere he asserts that "the influence of the Church is not likely to weaken in Ireland. But it will remain an influence that no lover of freedom can altogether approve" (125). Joyce's review of the book includes the observation that it formulates "a distinct accusation of English civilisation and English modes of thought" (*CW* 90); although this may be true, Gwynn's book also demonstrates his collusion in those modes of thought and, for that matter, in the modes of thought of many Irishmen, including Joyce himself. Those thought patterns reveal the Irish as passive sufferers of a great wound, succumbing to the influence of a Church that stifles the individual will.

An anonymous review of George Moore's *The Untilled Field* in the *Dublin Daily Express* of September 3, 1903, provides another example of the rhetoric pervasive during Joyce's last years of residence in Ireland. The reviewer insists that "these stories tell us that the Gael is disappearing from his native land because the priests have crushed the life out of him, have taken from him all the joy and beauty in life that his Celtic temperament craves for; and to have his manhood he goes to America where at least he can . . . have full play for his individuality. Some fifty thousand Roman Catholic peasants are leaving Ireland every year, and the reason for this despairing exodus Mr. Moore traces directly to the action of the priesthood."

This review, appearing alongside Joyce's "Aristotle on Education," is actually a far stronger indictment of the clergy than Moore submits in his stories. Moore depicts the clergy, as well as the laity, as caught in the net of the Famine's complicated aftermath. In "A Letter to Rome," a priest becomes so concerned about the diminishing population that he writes to the pope urging him to rescind the order for priestly celibacy: "Ireland was passing away. ... The remedy lies with the priesthood. If each priest were to take a wife about four thousand children would be born within the year ... in ten years Ireland would be saved by her priesthood" (179, 181). This passage neatly ties together the strands of the population problem in Ireland, emigration, celibacy, and religion.

Joyce knew *The Untilled Field* and very likely read the review of it in the *Daily Express*. Both support the emigrationist attitude apparent in his early writing: since conditions in Ireland could not support individuality, the only hope for survival was to escape. An alternative and widely held attitude was that although Ireland was still bleeding from the wound of the Famine, it could be regenerated if emigration were brought to a halt and the people of Ireland cooperated to heal and revive her. The Irish Literary Renaissance, the Gaelic League, the Land League, and the various agricultural cooperative movements all appealed to this instinct for communal survival through cooperative assertiveness. Paradoxically, the Famine provided a sort of charge for the cooperative movements just as it did for the individualists like Joyce. Plunkett, Gwynn, and Davitt all applaud and encourage the new spirit of cooperation, though each assesses the nature of the Irish "moral" character differently. They all look to the Famine for either incentive to reform or an explanation for Irish degeneracy which in turn calls for rebirth.

In *Contemporary Ireland,* published in 1907 in France and 1908 in Ireland, L. Paul-Dubois restates the case in favor of cooperation. He refutes Plunkett on several points and agrees with him on others; he praises Davitt highly and quotes from Daryl's book *Ireland's Disease.* The introduction to *Contemporary Ireland* was written by Thomas Kettle, Joyce's friend, schoolmate, and rival, who reviewed *Chamber Music* favorably but with some reservations about the lack of Irish tradition in the poems. Later, Kettle would frankly disapprove of the "unpatriotic candor" of *Dubliners* (Ellmann, *James Joyce* 63), Paul-Dubois would also have disapproved of the attitude of *Dubliners,* and *Portrait* as well, for he

looked upon emigration as a "bloodletting" to be staunched by such revitalizing forces as the Gaelic League and the Catholic religion to which,
he believed, the Irish people "instinctively" belonged (491).

Paul-Dubois deprecates "West Britons, as the phrase goes" (398)
and refutes those who "choose to represent Ireland as a priest-ridden
country" (489). (Simon Dedalus comes to mind.) The institutions to
which Paul-Dubois attributes the power of revitalizing the communal
spirit in Ireland are the very ones that fling out nets at the soul of Stephen Dedalus. While it would be difficult to argue that Paul-Dubois and
Joyce were responding directly to each other, it is clear that they, along
with Plunkett, Gwynn, and Davitt, were participating in the same debate. Arguing against the Anglicanization of Ireland, Paul-Dubois says
that the country "cannot, as it chooses, acquire the soul of another people by some national metempsychosis," but that the Gaelic League might
"regenerate its soul from within and teach Ireland how she can again be
a nation" (400, 402).

Stephen Dedalus—and Joyce—would choose to save Ireland from
without, by repressing the communal spirit, asserting individuality, and
creating a conscience for the nation. But that decision was made against
a tremendous drive for regeneration in 1904. In *James Joyce: The Undiscover'd Country,* Bernard Benstock notes that "Joyce tenaciously swam
against the current: at a time when a young Irish writer could finally feel
himself part of an indigenous literary movement . . . [Joyce] could not allow himself to accept a literary tradition that he considered primitive. . . .
To be a great writer meant . . . total commitment to the full development
of a world literary tradition" (*xiv*). One might say that Joyce opted to be
the medium for the dissemination of Irishness into that larger literary
ground. In his paper on Irish emigration, R. C. Geary concludes that
"emigration has given this country a vastly greater influence and pres-
tige in the world than the size of the home population would warrant. . . .
A world destiny is more glorious than a narrow parochial one" (8).
Geary's findings seem to vindicate Joyce's decision to leave Ireland (and,
incidentally, Bloom's position in "Cyclops").

As his emigration became permanent and his life more and more
complicated by personal relationships with Nora, their children, and the
publishing world, Joyce's engagements with population control naturally became more complex, more than an unconscious justification for
his own emigration. Both the facts of his life and the evidence in his fiction reveal that Joyce became increasingly interested in birth control.

Birth control was decidedly an issue in the early twentieth century. For all practical purposes, what has come to be called "the birth control movement" (often identified with the Malthusian League), began in London in 1876 in the wake of the highly publicized trial of Charles Bradlaugh and Annie Besant for the publication of an "obscene" pamphlet. Charles Knowlton's *Fruits of Philosophy* was a tract on family planning which had been available since 1830, but the trial gave the League and the birth control movement the kind of impetus they needed to propel them into a fifty-year campaign for "early marriage and normal sexual relations without the risk of pregnancy" (Soloway 55). The League president and his wife, like nearly all "neo-Malthusians," were freethinking, liberal utilitarians schooled in the political economics of Malthus, Adam Smith, and the two Mills. They succeeded in making birth control a national movement in England. Richard Brown points out that "Joyce evidently enjoyed the equivocal tone of the birth control movement, partly reformist and partly indecent [making] HCE support, among a variety of other liberal schemes, 'immaculate contraceptives for the populace' " (Brown 66; *FW* 45.14).

When the Malthusian League disbanded in 1927, it had published "well over three million pieces of literature and delivered thousands of lectures" (Soloway 55). Significant evidence of the success of the League might be read into the cautious "acceptance of 'methods' other than those of sexual abstinence to avoid parenthood" which was granted by the Anglican Church at the Lambeth Conference of 1930 (Noonan, "Contraception" 212). Meantime, in Ireland, the Censorship of Publications Act of 1929 made it a crime to print, publish, sell, or distribute "any book or periodical which advocates or might be supposed to advocate the unnatural prevention of conception" (Noonan, *Contraception* 411). And, on December 31, 1930, Pope Pius XI responded to the Resolutions of the Lambeth Conference with *Casti Connubii*, an encyclical that adamantly reasserts the Church's stand against artificial contraception.

Joyce owned several works expressing a variety of views on the subject of birth control, including Shaw's *Getting Married* and a Fabian tract, "The Decline in the Birth-Rate." Additionally, he had in his Trieste library two works that outlined the Church's objections to all "non-procreative sexuality" (see Brown 64). Just as the Church was implicated in Ireland's response to the Famine and the old Malthusianism, so was the Church perceived to be the cause of Ireland's response to the new Malthusians. Joyce's readings and writings demonstrate his interest in both the socioeconomic and religious interpretations of a subject which had for him not only demographic ramifications, but also deep personal and artistic significance. Before he was an artist, Joyce was a poor Irish Catholic Dubliner, the son of a woman who experienced seventeen pregnancies and died at the age of forty-five.

Mary Jane Murray Joyce represented an extreme case both of the already extremely high marital fertility rate of Irish women and of their relatively low life expectancy. The fertility record of the John Joyces brings to mind Bloom's observation of Simon Dedalus, "Fifteen children he had. Birth every year almost. That's in their theology. . . . Increase and multiply. Did you ever hear such an idea?" (*U* 151.36–40: *U* 8.31–33). Or Molly's scornful attitude toward Theodore Purefoy (whose theology and productivity Bloom seems not to question) for "filling [Mina] up with a child or twins once a year as regular as the clock" (*U* 742.24–25: *U* 18.160–61). Joyce's further personal involvement in birth control matters is indicated by certain facts in his own life; although they could ill-afford it, Joyce and Nora begot their first child almost immediately after their elopement in 1904, yet, as far as we know, Nora's last pregnancy occurred in 1908 and ended in miscarriage. It seems, therefore, that the Joyces practiced some form of contraception after that time, just as the Blooms had done since Rudy's death.

In *Ulysses* and the *Wake*, Joyce raises questions, which he does not finally answer, about the value and consequences of nonreproductive sexual activity. What Richard Brown calls the Blooms' "contraceptive sexual relationship" (67) might very well be the underlying cause of the entire action of Bloomsday—Bloom's nonconfrontation with Boylan and/or Molly—as well as a paradigm for twentieth-century society. As a contraceptive society, twentieth-century Western civilization is often forced, like the Blooms, to skirt certain issues. For example, it can be argued that when the procreative act as often as not becomes an end in itself, and becomes detached from regeneration, it is no longer logically or physically connected to the family, the traditional unit of society. Furthermore, if the primary purpose of sexuality is to provide pleasure and fulfillment to the participants (rather than to ensure the survival of the race), then it becomes difficult to argue against any sexual practice that is experienced as pleasurable; nor is a partner of the opposite sex, or any partner at all, absolutely necessary for sexual fulfillment. The very basis of communality was being called into question at the turn of the century, and Joyce participated in the discussion.

Both communal and individual birth control practices are extensively treated in all their complexity in "Oxen of the Sun." It is here that Joyce reveals the contradictory nature of Genesis 1:28–30, which paradoxically calls for fecundity and restraint. "Be fruitful and multiply, and replenish the earth," and, commands the God of Moses, "subdue it." This mandate, along with the passage on Onan in Genesis 38:9–10, shaped Judaic thinking about population control. Christian attitudes, rooted in these two doctrines, became somewhat complicated by the example of a celibate (though sensuous) God-man who insisted that his followers must love one another. Joyce exploits the inherent contradictions in these precepts for all they are worth in "Oxen" and again in the *Wake*, demonstrating how the natural tendency to re-create and sustain oneself (as individual, family, nation, work of art) is always subdued (modified, that is, not completely frustrated) by a counterforce which gathers its strength from the original tendency. Thus, the lying-in hospital of "Oxen" is the scene of a birth and a parody of the Last Supper where the apostles become drunken bachelors. The Church, in its stand on reproduction, is both bully and bulldozed. The Oxen of the title represent all the victims in the episode—Ireland, the diseased cattle, Bloom, Stephen, the wasted seed of the revelers, and so on—and yet the oxen themselves provide the very means, the oxengut, from which a condom can be made, whereby the crime of contraception can be perpetrated.

The mandate of Genesis both demands fecundity and is itself fertile, for it engenders innumerable interpretations leading to questions about the increase and multiplication, not only of food and bodies, but of ideas and language. Similarly, Malthus's "Essay on Population," in many ways a caution against Genesis, has been astonishingly productive. Seven variations of the essay were published between 1798 and 1872 ("Population Ethics," 1234); it was invoked by political economists to justify nonintervention in the Famine and by the neo-Malthusians to justify the use of contraceptive devices (though Malthus himself called for "moral restraint"). In his autobiography, Darwin even credits Malthus with providing the "primary stimulus" for the concept of natural selection (Keynes 360). Joyce advertises his ambition in "Oxen" by embedding the Genesis passage in the opening page of the episode and then engaging it in conflict with several variations of the Malthusian theme. The result is a literary tour de force which cuts across the multiple conflicting dimensions of political, scientific, and religious interpretations of population control. Underlying all the views represented in the discourse are problems of sexuality and the survival of the family and community. Joyce exposes all of those problems. (In chapter 3, I will discuss at length the complex issues of population control raised in "Oxen.")

As the birth control movement progressed into the second decade of the twentieth century, it gained momentum, picking up resistance and converts along the way. Charges were brought against the neo-Malthusians by both religious and political organizations (notably the Catholic church and the French government) for being antifamily. In response, the organization redefined itself from one which promulgated birth control to one which advocated "family planning." The difference between Joyce's emphasis in *Ulysses* and in *Finnegans Wake* might be roughly characterized the same way. As Shari Benstock points out, "when we are introduced to Mr. and Mrs. Porter, we learn 'They care for nothing except everything that is allporterous' " (250).

In the *Wake*, Joyce examines familial relationships in order to discover how they will withstand and prevail over the pressures of the twentieth century, including, among others, those exerted by the new sexuality and its implicit new morality. With regard to the breakup of the family, once again, Joyce had in the Famine a generator of attitudes at his command. During the Famine, the destruction of the family had been a major concern, not just for those who lost members through death, but also for those who saw their relatives off to new worlds. From the point of view of those remaining in Ireland, the emigrants might as well have been dying, and the custom that developed to mourn their loss clearly has relevance for the *Wake*. Gallagher describes the phenomenon at length: "On the night before the departing one was scheduled to make the trip to port and board ship, the family held what later became known as an 'American Wake,' a custom unique to Ireland" (122). The American Wake was variously called the "farewell supper," "live wake," "convoy," or "American bottle night" (122). It was an evening spent in "somber discussion of the United States," a final offer of advice from the old to the departing youth.

Everyone had some advice to contribute at the American Wake, "but given the Irishmen's facility of speech . . . and his ability to embellish, alter, and distort, an actual letter from America, raised high like a prize . . . then re-opened for the hundredth time . . . and finally read aloud," was considered the most authentic and reliable source of information about the nature of the emigrant's future life (129). The Famine, the emigration, and the resulting changes in the population of Ireland "soured" the memories of the elders and "set them to wondering about what they had thought were eternal verities" (131). The American Wake, therefore, elicited a variety of conflicting emotions, for, "if departure was a kind of death, so was being left with the conviction that your country and way of life were finished. . . . The evening gradually became cathartic for everyone except the intending emigrant. . . . Like a man attending his own funeral, the emigrant seemed to be trying more and more desperately to relate what was happening to him to something habitual in the past that his imagination might at least pursue. . . . As the night wore on, his relationship with . . . his own parents, brothers and sisters, became faultless, even ideal, for being in the very process of ceasing to exist" (132).

Again, Famine rhetoric contributes to a prevailing discourse of the twentieth century, that of the dissolution of the family, and the *Wake* demonstrates the influence of both the older and the newer discussions. Many of the important elements in the American Wake are significant features of *Finnegans Wake:* the letter (in the *Wake* one of the most important versions of the letter comes from Boston), the death that is not a death, the dreamlike awareness of transformations taking place on a global scale. The history of population control, like "Oxen" and the *Wake,* is an "allincluding most farraginous chronicle" (*U* 423.26: *U* 14.1412) covering as it does the debates about the manipulation of the fertility, mortality, and migration of the human race.

The machinations of population politics were fairly well concealed, or at least seem to have gone unnoticed in the Western world, until political economics began openly to pressure population growth in the eighteenth and nineteenth centuries. The place where population was conceived—the sexual act—came under unflinching scrutiny sometime between 1800 and 1900, thereby providing tremendous force to the deployment of sexuality which continues to this day. Joyce responds in his own particular voice to the discourses on population control, but that voice draws at least a portion of its energy from the reverberations of the Great Famine, an event that had an impact on every feature of the Irish population.

2

The Urge to Emigrate

"In February, 1847, the headlong flight from Ireland began"
—Cecil Woodham-Smith, *The Great Hunger* 215.

During the years when Joyce was growing to young manhood, one of the first things to attract the eye of a visitor in Ireland was a ubiquitous, gaudy poster depicting a ship under full sail and advocating "Emigration!" (Daryl 184). In 1901, Ireland lost one of every 114 members of its population, while Italy, Scotland, Norway, and Spain lost one in 200 or more, and other European countries lost fewer than one per 400 of population. By 1904, when the Irish renaissance and the various cooperative movements were underway, an Anti-Emigration Society had been formed to reverse the trend (Paul-Dubois 357, 361). The popular aspiration was then, and remained into the 1930s, a return to the pre-Famine population level of 8.5 million (Geary 7). Virtually every type of text produced in or about Ireland in the last decade of the nineteenth and the first several decades of the twentieth century—journal article, novel, history, sermon, and, judging from "Cyclops," even barroom declamation—reflected, however subtly, the concern about depopulation. Like the subject of emigration itself, the tendency to assign blame and prescribe a remedy was irrepressible.

Joyce's references to emigration in his critical writings reveal his typically Irish preoccupation with the subject and a thorough familiarity with its history; these references also expose Joyce's attempt to present his case in favor of the emigrant. He accurately cites current emigration statistics in "Ireland, Island of Saints and Sages," including in his account the recurrent metaphor of Ireland as an anemic and dying body: "The

poor, anaemic, almost lifeless body lies in agony, the rulers give orders
and the priests administer last rites" (*CW* 172). In the same essay he repeats a common contention that

> when the Irishman is found outside of Ireland in another environ-
> ment, he very often becomes a respected man. The economic and
> intellectual conditions that prevail in his own country do not permit
> the development of individuality ... [I]ndividual initiative is para-
> lysed by the influence and admonitions of the church. ... No one
> who has any self-respect stays in Ireland, but flees afar as though
> from a country that has undergone the visitation of an angered Jove.
> (*CW* 171)

Here, Joyce states in direct terms what he will insist on more artistically
in *Dubliners* and *Portrait:* that the individual who respects himself and
seeks respect from others must resist the reproaches of the Church and
leave Ireland. Away from home, Irish men and women have the opportunity of fulfilling their potential; at home, there is no hope.

Declan Kiberd observes that "in his published work, the young
Joyce liked to offer high-falutin' explanations of his flight from the nets
of nationality, language and religion, but the real reasons were probably
a good deal more practical and economic" (2). The "high-falutin" explanations to which Kiberd refers are surely apparent in Joyce's work, but
so are the practical ones. The genteel poverty represented by the "new
secondhand clothes" that Stephen's mother packs for him just before he
leaves the country, for example, offsets the pomposity of Stephen's intention "to forge ... the uncreated conscience of [his] race" (*P* 252–53).
In fact, practical, artistic, and psychological defenses of emigration run
through all of Joyce's works. But one of the most persistent among the
many types of defenses, especially in his early works, is the contention
that the Church has created conditions that make life in Ireland unbearable. For example, in the passage from "Ireland, Island of Saints and
Sages" quoted above, a passage meant to explain why "no one who has
any self-respect stays in Ireland," there is a restatement of the argument
of "The Sisters," even to the use of the word "paralysed." When Joyce
says that "individual initiative is paralysed by the influence and admo-
nitions of the church," he might easily be talking about Father Flynn as
both victim and carrier of the Church's immobilizing infection.

In "Fenianism," Joyce establishes as a "backdrop" to the "sad com-
edy" of nationalist and Fenian rivalry,

the spectacle of a population which diminishes year by year with mathematical regularity, of the uninterrupted emigration to the United States or Europe of Irishmen for whom the economic and intellectual conditions of their native land are unbearable. And almost as if to set in relief this depopulation there is a long parade of churches, cathedrals, convents, monasteries and seminaries to tend the spiritual needs of those who have been unable to find courage or money enough to undertake the voyage from Queenstown to New York. (*CW* 190)

Here, Joyce reiterates the economic and intellectual rationale for emigration offered in "Ireland, Island of Saints and Sages," and adds to self-respect (which he previously stressed) another characteristic of the emigrant: courage, a virtue unknown among his Dubliners, who represent the variety of Irish men and women who stayed behind.

Joyce fortifies his case against the Church as a cause of emigration by depicting the "spectacle of the world in thrall" to the Church. That spectacle fills Stephen, who is more courageous than his fellow Dubliners, with "the fire of courage" to leave Ireland (*SH* 194). Like Father Flynn, who depends on the charity of his sisters, the Church that Joyce represents in "Fenianism" lives parasitically on the meager earnings of the faithful who would be better off to forsake their faith or practice it elsewhere. The somewhat strained connection Joyce makes between emigration and expenditures for Church buildings in the quotation above may owe something to Horace Plunkett's *Ireland in the New Century*. Plunkett notes in Ireland "the multiplication—in inverse ratio to a declining population—of costly and elaborate monastic and conventual institutions, involving what in the aggregate must be an enormous annual expenditure" (108).

Joyce points out, in "Ireland at the Bar," that "there are twenty million Irishmen scattered all over the world. The Emerald Isle contains only a small part of them. ... six centuries of armed occupation and more than a hundred years of English legislation ... [have] reduced the population of the unhappy island from eight to four million" (*CW* 199). Elsewhere in the essay Joyce refers to "the real sovereign of Ireland, the Pope" who consistently decides in favor of English interests over Irish ones. By designating the pope a sovereign, Joyce reinforces the link between oppressive living conditions and the Church in Ireland. In *Portrait* particularly, Joyce makes the Church the final cause of nearly all Irish identity problems. He argues that the Church has imposed on Ireland a false conscience, a perverted moral faculty that has rendered the nation incapable of dealing realistically with the question of survival (or as Stephen calls it, "life").

In *Stephen Hero,* Stephen likens the influence of Catholicism to a plague of vermin "begotten in the catacombs in an age of sickness and cruelty. ... every natural impulse towards health and wisdom and happiness had been corroded by the pest of these vermin" (*SH* 194). Stephen's choice of metaphor recalls Michael Davitt's description of the Irish during the Famine, "so dead to every sense and right of manhood were the Irish people reduced in these black years of hopeless life and of a fetid pestilence of perverted morality" (47).

The immediate, specific result of the threat of the Church's contaminating influence as represented in *Portrait* is Stephen's decision to leave the country. The larger-scale consequence of the "plague of Catholicism," as Joyce and other writers have represented it, is emigration itself. Even in *Ulysses,* where Joyce's antagonism toward the Church seems to have softened, the Church–emigration link is discernible. In "Oxen," according to "Mr Stephen," the "men of the island," unable to compete with the priests for the attentions of "the ungrate women" (and as if responding to the advice of that gaudy poster described at the opening of this chapter), "loaded themselves and their bundles of chattels on shipboard, set all masts erect, manned the yards, sprang their luff, heaved to, spread three sheets in the wind ... and put to sea to recover the main of America" (*U* 401.18–25: *U* 14.640–46).

Joyce argued candidly for emigration in his critical writings, but the subtle statements in his fiction are more impressive. The later works treat the subject with humor, but *Dubliners* and *Portrait* take it very seriously. Deborah M. Averill discovers in the Irish short story of the renaissance period "two antithetical viewpoints on Irish life" which coincide with popular conflicting attitudes toward emigration. Averill finds that "the stories of Moore and Joyce reflect a feeling of hopelessness about Ireland's future and a belief that escape from the country is necessary for personal fulfillment [while] O'Kelly and Corkery ... express ... a spirit of national reawakening and a strong feeling for Ireland as a nurturing home. ... Emigration and exile were important facts of the Irish national experience. ... individuals sometimes [sought] permanent escape from the community, but not without intense inner conflict" (24).

In the remainder of this chapter, I will focus on "The Sisters," "Eveline," and *Portrait* in examining the pressures that prompted Joyce to explain and defend his urge to emigrate and his complex means of making that defense. The texts of these works encompass not only the definitive editions published by Viking, but also, in the case of "The Sisters," the version published in the *Irish Homestead* as well as the *Homestead* itself and the ongoing debate about Irish emigration. In the case of *Portrait,* the 1914 edition will be considered both as part of the volumes of the *Egoist* in which it first appeared and in the larger context of what Foucault calls the deployment of sexuality. In *Portrait,* sexuality becomes interrelated with the subject of the Church's repressive role in Ireland. Influenced by attitudes generated in the international discussion of sexual norms, Joyce and other writers such as George Moore incorporated these attitudes into their own cultural documents, making the need to overcome what appeared to be typically Irish misconceptions about sexual morality a significant cause of emigration.

In addition to demonstrating the interplay of the texts of "The Sisters" and *Portrait* with each other and with their various modifications and extensions, I will refer frequently to the same resonant histories of Ireland called on previously. Since the works of Daryl, Plunkett, Davitt, and Paul-Dubois have received and echoed many of the cultural vibrations affecting Joyce's works, they show clearly how one text invades another, ransacks its contents, and appropriates the spoils.

Critics generally agree that Joyce's fiction is to some extent a defense of his own behavior. In *Portrait,* the reader follows the author-hero's stand-in, Stephen Dedalus, as he attempts to disentangle himself from the bonds of family, Church, and nation. Since Stephen cannot get free of these apparently sinister attachments in Ireland, the reader agrees that Stephen, like Joyce, must leave the country. In *Dubliners,* on the other hand, the hero literally stands *out;* he is conspicuous by his absence. Those who are present seem incapable of escape; in one way or another, they are all paralyzed. The reader feels pity at best, contempt at worst, for the demoralized population of Dublin: Father Flynn, Eveline, Little Chandler, Maria, Gabriel Conroy, and the rest. The courageous Dubliner, the one the reader would respect and who respects himself, has left.

Helene Cixous, too, finds that the negative characteristics and behaviors of Joyce's Dubliners set the virtues of a missing hero in relief. She views *Dubliners* as an "antiportrait, a series of images to which Joyce opposes the positive features of his own personality" (264). Those features will come clear in the *Portrait.* Similarly, Florence Walzl finds that *Dubliners* and *Portrait* "complement each other. They are like the two faces of some ancient coin: on one side is the picture of the city, and on the other, the profile of the hero." Walzl also observes that both *Dubliners* and *Portrait* "present vindications of Joyce's self-imposed exile" (167, 168).

In the final, 1906 modification of "The Sisters," Joyce sets the tone for *Dubliners* and previews the *Portrait*. He insures that the reader will excuse the young narrator for feeling relieved at the death of a paralytic, "too scrupulous" old priest. Father Flynn, who represents the allegedly defective and docile conscience of Ireland, had captivated the boy's imagination. But because of the meticulously executed and increasingly malignant picture of the priest that develops in the story, the reader does not blame the narrator for relishing his freedom from the sick old man, even though "he had taught [him] a great deal" (*D* 13). Likewise, the reader does not blame—and therefore excuses and accepts the apology of—Stephen Dedalus for happily releasing himself from the moral perversions of his Church, nation, and family even though they had been the sources of all his learning.

After rejecting the director's suggestion of a vocation in *Portrait*, Stephen feels a sense of wonder "at the frail hold which so many years of order and obedience had of him when once a definite and irrevocable act of his threatened to end for ever, in time and in eternity, his freedom" (*P* 161–62). Stephen's wonder is analogous to the response of the young narrator of "The Sisters" who "found it strange that neither I nor the day seemed in a mourning mood and I felt even annoyed at discovering in myself a sensation of freedom" (*D* 12). The unattractive rendering of the Irish Jesuit that gradually materializes in *Portrait* especially parallels the formulation of Father Flynn. In each case the priest develops into the symbol of a sterile morality that determines the hero's rejection of a vocation.

In the original published text of "The Sisters," the priest is not paralyzed and the boy discovers no "sensation of freedom as if [he] had been freed from something by [the priest's] death" (*D* 12). Neither is the reader informed at the outset that there is "no hope" (*D* 9). *Gnomon* and *simony* do not haunt the boy's imagination, nor does he dream of the priest's confession. All of these additions appear in the final paradigmatic version, which was completed after Joyce had emigrated and his need to defend his decision had become almost one with his artistic mission. At this time Joyce was in the early stages of what he would come to call his self-exile, a state nonetheless parallel to the condition of the emigrant. The recent emigrant typically experiences (simultaneously) longing for and rejection of his or her homeland. In fact, it is important that the emigrant cultivate the tendency to reject his or her old home in order to sustain the purpose of building a new life. In time, the rejection is often transformed into fond memories. Certainly Joyce's admission that he may have painted too harsh a picture of Dubliners in his short stories and his consequent decision to highlight the hospitality of his people in "The Dead" (Ellmann, *James Joyce* 254) reflects such a transformation—even if considerably modified—from bitter to fond memories. The representation of the Dublin Irish that emerges in *Ulysses* also suggests to some extent that Joyce's attitude had become more balanced.

Each of the particular additions and modifications in "The Sisters," however, serves to align its theme with the attitude about Ireland's potential that Joyce articulates in the critical writings quoted above, which were written in 1907, just after Joyce had established himself as an emigrant. The reader tends to feel as George Bernard Shaw did about the question of Joyce's fixations on Dublin. Kiberd reports that Shaw "could fully understand why James Joyce should wish to leave such a dreary place, but not why he should want to recall it in such meticulous detail in his works" (Kiberd 1).

By way of a partial answer, I suggest that the current of the discourse on Ireland's population pressured Catholics to be extraordinarily defensive because their religion was implicated in the "crime" of emigration at so many points of the investigation. To those who believed, as Joyce did, that the Church had formed (or rather mis-formed) the conscience of the nation, the Church was responsible for all of Ireland's moral decisions, and these decisions determined its political as well as its spiritual behavior. The downfall of Parnell as represented in *Portrait*, for example, is ultimately attributable to the misguidance of the Church.

Individually, the Catholic citizen was forced to measure all of his or her actions against the standards of the Church. Even today, as Kevin O'Reilly points out, "Catholicism is so pervasive in Ireland that the Church has influence in secular areas as well. The Church has long enjoyed a quasi-'state religion' status in Ireland. Until 1972, a clause in the Constitution [December 1921] prohibited any laws which contravened the laws of the Catholic Church" (225). Before 1921, these prohibitions were unwritten but equally binding on the Irish citizen.

The Church joined forces with the various cooperative movements in Ireland early in this century in actively preaching and working against emigration. Even when the organization was not a religiously affiliated one, as in the case of the Gaelic League or Horace Plunkett's Irish Agricultural Organisation Society, it shared at least one concern with the Church—to stop the national "bloodletting." Paul-Dubois records that the Catholic clergy played an active role in the newly-formed Anti-Emigration Society, for example (361). An article appearing in the "Ireland" section of the May 30, 1904, *London Times* further illustrates the point: "The people of Enniscorthy held a public meeting on Thursday for the purpose of taking steps to start an industry that will provide local employment and stop emigration. There was a large attendance of clergy and laity of all denominations" (10). Father Healy, a priest who appears briefly in *Stephen Hero*, is just the sort of clergyman who would have attended that meeting. Having recently returned from America, where he had spent seven years raising money to build a new chapel near Enniscorthy, he "was greatly interested in the new Gaelic revival and in the new literary movement in Ireland" (157).

The rhetorical pressures about emigration imposed on the Irish generally are also evident in various parts of the August 13, 1904, *Irish Homestead*, where the first published version of "The Sisters" appeared. On page 663 of that edition is recorded the news that the members of the Ancient Order of Hibernians in America "rejoice in the efforts now being made to revivify the interests of Ireland ... thereby stemming the tide of emigration so fast depopulating her shores." Ironically, the support of the emigrants themselves had been enlisted in the war against emigration. Their cooperation was easily gained, because the Irish who had left shared in the "national guilt complex" which contributed to the Irish sense of tragedy about emigration (Geary 4).

The most interesting of the contributions surrounding "The Sisters" in the *Irish Homestead* is located in the "Household Hints" column on page 674. The circuitous route it takes to reach its conclusion—that the Irish should stay in Ireland and buy Irish products—and the bizarre associations it makes along the way reflect an extraordinarily complex view about the responsibility of the citizen for the survival of the country. Many of the attitudes and fears expressed in the article are satirized, parodied, or otherwise addressed in Joyce's works.

The writer begins by recounting the story of a man who attempted to open a business and met with nothing but indifference. The author contends that such indifference to native enterprise is both typical of the Irish and threatening to "Irish possibilities." Next, women come under direct attack from the author for fantasizing about an "ideal world ... in which there [are] no consequences." Those women would do better to face the reality of Irish life, the author believes, and change its conditions if need be. In *Stephen Hero*, May Dedalus explains to Stephen that she "would like to read some great writer, to see what ideal of life he has—amn't I right in saying 'ideal'? ... Because sometimes ... I feel I want to leave this actual life and enter another—for a time" (85–86). What is particularly upsetting to the author of the *Homestead* piece is the possibility that women with such a "haphazard outlook on life" will pass that view on to their children. There is no such danger where Stephen Dedalus is concerned, of course, for it is the real world which beckons to him, and he replies to his mother, "That is wrong; that is the mistake everyone makes. Art is not an escape from life!" (86).

To establish her point about the need for cooperative effort in Ireland, the author of "Household Hints" cites emigration statistics:

> Irishmen and women, who have just been informed through the public press, treating of the vital statistics of Ireland, that in the decennial period ending in 1900 the population of Ireland diminished by a quarter of a million; yet knowing this, and having it in their power to staunch this outflow of the remaining life-blood of a nation that has already been bled white, will not make the smallest effort to do so, although every single man and woman remaining in the country can help at least a little, and if everyone helped, this co-operation would in itself make a new Ireland.

Like the Irish men and women the author mentions, Joyce had been informed of the vital statistics of Ireland. He quoted them frequently in his critical writings and put them into the mouth of the Citizen. This use of statistics reflects the growing tendency in Western culture to use numbers as authority or justification for various attitudes, policies, or actions. That statistics were often considered to be "vital," even when applied to a country rather than a body, suggests not only that they indicated trends in patterns of habitation, but that they were perceived somehow to have the power to *affect* life and determine survival. Nearly all the historians I have quoted repeat, with slight variations, the statistics of the Famine and emigration, and the more current the history, the more obvious is the use of statistics to reach conclusions about Ireland's prospects and recommended courses of action.

Foucault suggests that demography itself, which relies heavily on the analysis of statistics and which emerged as a science in the nineteenth century, represents a form of population control (*History of Sexuality* 140). To increase the affective value of the statistics of emigration, the "Household Hints" author combines them with the anemia metaphor, implementing a rhetorical practice apparently standard in Ireland since the Famine. Daryl, Kettle, Gwynn, Davitt, Paul-Dubois, and Joyce all subscribe to it.

After recounting the vital statistics of Ireland, the author of "Household Hints" reveals another concern about "national decay," related to the problem of emigration: "There are ... unfriended districts in the country where an able-bodied man is now hardly to be found, but only the aged and young boys ... the crippled and diseased, physically and mentally—these last a contingent with whose unhappy lives is involved a more and more pressing question of unspeakable national menace." The author's comments seem to corroborate and underscore the insinuations made several pages later in "The Sisters" about Father Flynn's "affected" mind, his not very intelligent sisters, and their influence on the mind of the young narrator.

Both the "Household Hints" observations and the insinuations in "The Sisters" reflect the growing national awareness of the unusually high incidence of "lunacy" in Ireland. One theory held that the increase was brought on by the fact that the healthiest of the population had been emigrating steadily since the Famine. "We have another grave sign of racial decadence [in] the marked increase of mental disease during the last fifty years" (Paul-Dubois 364). As Stephen is riding out to Mullingar in *Stephen Hero*, the driver of the trap points out the lunatic asylum "and added impressively that there were a great many patients in it" (*SH* 239). In *Contemporary Ireland*, Paul-Dubois observes that "An Anglo-Irish Protestant, Mr. Filson Young, author of *Ireland at the Crossroads* (London, 1904, p. 117, etc.), believes that the true cause of the increase in mental disease is Roman Catholicism. ... We merely note the fact in order to show how far prejudice may carry some minds" (365). Joyce increases the sense of Father Flynn's physical and mental handicaps in the final version of "The Sisters," achieving a mood like the "unspeakable national menace" referred to by the "Household Hints" contributor. Thus does a concern in one section of the *Homestead* seem to have rewritten another.

The final portion of the "Household Hints" column returns the reader's attention to Irish women, whose share in the reclamation of the country is to buy Irish products to the exclusion of all others. The author claims to "have known housekeepers who habitually use imported soap" in spite of the fact that Irish soap is cheaper. (In "Lestrygonians," Bloom remembers, "American soap I bought: elderflower" [*U* 155.37: *U* 8.172].) The type of thoughtless and unpatriotic behavior indulged in by housekeepers who buy imported soap is "a small illustration" for the author of "Household Hints" of a "want of heart, or, what amounts to the same thing, conscience, that is disquieting in the present critical time of Irish history ... a survival of the timid and servile spirit superinduced in an evil age that ought to be lived down by now."

The author's reference to the lack of conscience in Ireland brings to mind Stephen's mission at the end of *Portrait* to forge the uncreated conscience of his race, while the allusion to the Famine points in innumerable directions at once. For one, it points back to page 663 of the same edition of the *Homestead*, where a letter to the editor reminds the reader that "we took the Famine of '46 lying down; we allowed its victims to starve and die." The correspondent goes on to suggest that if Irish workers are to compete in the labor market, they must keep pace with the times, come out from under the influence of the Famine, improve the environment, "or make room for the strong." The invocation of the Famine as a reproach against weakness and passivity is familiar by now. Kettle, Davitt, Daryl, and Paul-Dubois all used it.

Clearly, the contributors to the *Homestead*, like the authors of the various contemporary histories of Ireland that I have cited, based their pleas for cooperation during Ireland's current "crisis" partly on the memory of the Famine, which, though it was a communal experience, did not elicit effective cooperative resistance. Attitudes expressed in Irish short stories are also deeply rooted in perceptions of the national experience. According to Averill, "the genre evolved in response to the peculiar frustrations and conflicts of Irish life" (3). One of the peculiarly frustrating experiences that Averill pinpoints is "the catastrophic Famine which . . . produced drastic changes in Irish society and created a cultural void that lasted for the next half century" (11). In *The Irish Novelists: 1800–1850*, Thomas Flanagan substantiates Averill's observations about the Famine: "In the years which followed 1850, the despair was universal. . . . the island accepted passively the nightmare of its history. Seen in this context, Joyce's *non serviam* is less the mutinous refusal of the artist to accept social responsibility than the necessary assertion of individuality against the abnormal claims imposed by a particular culture" (336).

Joyce's first short story seems to invoke the Famine, at least indirectly, for if we are to believe the death notice pinned to the crape— "July 1st, 1895 . . . aged sixty-five years" (*D* 12)—Father Flynn spent his adolescence during the Famine, when typhus, cholera, and other forms of pestilence were rampant and when the incidence of "lunacy" in Ireland began to increase. Furthermore, like the Famine victims who remained in Ireland and refrained from "stealing" the grain marked for the landlords, Father Flynn was "too scrupulous always" (17), and also like them, he was "peaceful and resigned" to death (15).

Ellmann tells us that in 1906 and 1907 Joyce "kept plaguing [his] Aunt Josephine . . . for copies of everything to do with Ireland, particularly newspapers but also magazines and books. Irish history continued to fascinate him" (*James Joyce* 236). It seems likely that the frequent direct and indirect references in these histories and journals to the Famine and the consequent emigration contributed to the "special odour of corruption" of "The Sisters" and helped to turn it into the opening of his "chapter on the moral history" of his country (*L 1*, 123, 135). The exact influences on Joyce's text are impossible to pin down, but so is the text itself. Does "The Sisters" begin in the "death of the old, paralyzed, and demented priest to whom [Joyce] was related on his mother's side" (Ellmann, *James Joyce* 163) and end in the "final" version published by Viking? Is it reconsidered, and to some extent rewritten and expanded, in *Portrait*, where the picture of the malignant Irish Catholic priest is more subtly and effectively drawn? The boundaries of "The Sisters" are difficult to find when the story is placed in the rhetorical and ideological milieu that pressured it into existence.

An examination of Joyce's use of the word *paralysis* in "The Sisters," for example, especially demands the breaking down of textual boundaries. Its effect on the narrator of the story and on the reader is to raise the question, "What *else* is meant by this word?" If the reader then begins to examine the documents written in and about Ireland during the composition of "The Sisters," he or she begins to note that *paralysis* incorporates definitions and connotations relating to events and attitudes surrounding the Famine and the emigration that followed it. Certainly those critics are correct who find that the italicized words in the opening paragraph of the 1906 version of "The Sisters"—*paralysis, simony,* and *gnomon*—represent the three main themes of *Dubliners,* and clearly *paralysis* represents "the pathological inability of the characters to act purposefully" (Walzl 207). These themes did not become clear in Joyce's mind, however, until after he had left Ireland and had begun to turn the rhetoric of national survival against itself in order to establish a case for emigration. The word *paralysis* and its various connotations were readily available in the stock of responses about Ireland's plight. Several diseases, including paralysis, had been attributed to Irish society before, during, and after the final composition of "The Sisters," and such attributions were most often made with the intention of exposing Ireland's ills in order to cure them. Thus Joyce drew on a popular and long-standing rhetorical convention, one which gained force and frequency after the Famine, during which Ireland was, in fact, desperately and universally diseased.

Paul-Dubois reports that as early as 1727, Swift had referred to Ireland as "a patient" for whom England sent medicine and "had it applied by a doctor who knew neither the patient nor the malady." After the imposition of the Penal Laws and the resulting abortive insurrections in the early nineteenth century, Sheil had pronounced the country "palsied to the heart" (quoted in Paul-Dubois 54, 57). The Famine then etched even more deeply the already clear impression of Ireland as an invalid.

Famine rhetoric would eventually be translated into representations of social conditions as, for example, in the case of *Ireland's Disease.* Phillippe Daryl wrote the 1888 account of his impressions of Ireland for "the redress of Irish wrongs [that] can only come out of a sincere and assiduous exposure of the real state of affairs, which is not healthy but pathological [and] manifests itself by peculiar symptoms. ... Social war is still there, filling the hearts, paralyzing the action, poisoning the springs of life" (2).

Horace Plunkett carries on the tradition of exposing Ireland's afflictions in the preface to *Ireland in the New Century,* where he declares that his purpose is to reveal and suggest ways to overcome "certain defects of character" in the Irish which are "economically paralysing." Plunkett continues, "I need hardly say I refer to the lack of moral courage, initiative, independence and self-reliance—defects which, however they may be accounted for, it is the first duty of modern Ireland to recognize and overcome." Elsewhere in the book, Plunkett defines the "problem before us" as "how to make headway in view of the weakness of character to which I have had to attribute the paralysis of our activities in the past" (165). Plunkett's list of character defects might well be an inventory of the vices of Joyce's Dubliners. Later in the book Plunkett remarks on the "paralyzing effects of a system of land tenure." Thus, in his various uses of the word, Plunkett makes the Irish, as Joyce makes Father Flynn, both cause and victim of their own paralysis.

Declan Kiberd reports that when Plunkett suggested that economic development "was hampered by a lack of self-reliance in the national character, the prelates of the Catholic Church lashed out against the implications that they had weakened the independence of the Irish mind" (21). Kiberd's account demonstrates the attitudes prevalent in Ireland when both Plunkett and Joyce were attempting to raise the consciousness and the conscience of the nation; it seems also to justify Joyce's early belief that it would be impossible to do so given the nature of the nationalist movement and the power of the Church. Whether or not Joyce read Plunkett or Daryl, it is certain that Joyce's intention to "write a chapter of the moral history" of Ireland and his claim to the absolute truth, objectivity, and salutary purpose of his task were not unusual. Joyce's "scrupulous meanness" and his temerity about altering or deforming "what he has seen and heard" (*L* 2, 134) are surely prefigured by Daryl's "sincere and assiduous exposure of the real state of affairs" and matched by Plunkett's performance of "the first duty of modern Ireland to recognize and overcome" its defective moral character. All three men chose to represent the "truth" through the metaphor of paralysis. The difference is that Joyce did not believe Ireland could heal itself by internal cooperative effort. The critical reception of Plunkett's book suggests that Joyce's pessimism was, at least in the short term, well-founded.

Davitt speaks several times of attempts made by various parties to "paralyze" the action of the Land League (319, 339), and Stephen Gwynn describes the Ireland of Miss Edgeworth as "an Ireland lying as if in paralysis, vegetant rather than alive" (3). It is clear, then, that nearly every association of the word *paralysis* was available to Joyce in the histories and commentaries on Ireland that he read before and after he left the country. Joyce's interest in medicine, the traces of which Florence Walzl discerns in all of his works (158), may have made him particularly sensitive to the nuances of *paralysis,* but the analogy of Ireland to a victim of some crippling power was there for the borrowing and remained in currency after publication of "The Sisters." Paul-Dubois describes England's policy during the Famine: "England then undertook, with a selfishness for which the dominant mercantile theories of that day form but a poor excuse, to paralyse, and finally to destroy the industry and the commerce of Ireland" (321).

Just as paralysis became a common metaphor for Ireland's political, economic, and cultural condition, so did "the untilled field" take on a variety of connotations suggesting physical, economic, and cultural sterility. Daryl indicates that a "striking peculiarity of the scenery in Ireland is the scarcity of cultivated fields. . . . one thing surprises in those endless pastures—it is to count so few grazing beasts on them" (55–56). Plunkett devotes an entire chapter to "The Untilled Fields." And Davitt, replacing description with metaphor, designates social discontent in Ireland as "a vast untilled field of popular force, if its resource could only be drawn upon for the purposes of a national movement" (121). In the December 17, 1904, issue of the *Irish Homestead* there appears, along with Joyce's "After the Race," the continuation of an article on "Untilled Ground."

In George Moore's volume of short stories, *The Untilled Field,* which in many ways anticipated *Dubliners,* the sterile ground is symbolic of the depopulated country as well as the deficient moral courage of the peasants, who have been oppressed by the sanctions of the Church. Magalaner and Kain suggest that "though Joyce could learn little from the diction and style of Moore, he may have picked up and used several themes

that pervade *The Untilled Field*. Moore is fond of stressing the great influence of the none too scrupulous members of the clergy, the ignorance of
the ordinary Irishman, and the necessity of flight by emigration" (22–
23). But while some of Moore's peasants manage to leave Ireland, Joyce's
Dubliners all lack the courage.

The character in *Dubliners* who comes closest to making the break
for freedom is Eveline, the failed heroine of the second of the three
stories appearing in the *Homestead*. Just a month before Joyce himself
emigrated, he depicted with great perception the psychological conflict
of a young Dubliner on the verge of leaving her country for good. In his
analysis of "Eveline," Martin Dolch argues that the subject of escape
"must have occupied [Joyce's] mind a great deal, and it is indeed a problem that has long been of central importance to the Irish nation. Eveline is faced with the question whether or not to escape by emigration
from . . . a kind of life that drove her mother crazy. . . . Emigration, it appears, offers the only way to salvation. . . . in a personal way *Dubliners*
also gave Joyce an opportunity to state his reasons for exile and to justify
it before himself and before the world" (98, 101).

Just as Dolch has picked up on the signals sent out in "Eveline," so
must the subscribers to the *Irish Homestead* have done, for the newspaper
began receiving "many letters of complaint from readers in both the
country and the city" (Ellmann, *James Joyce* 165). Although in suggesting
that Joyce write for the *Homestead*, Russell had asked for something "live-
making . . . so as not to shock the readers" (*L* 2, 43), Joyce does nothing
in "Eveline" to suggest even the possibility of a satisfying, happy life in
Ireland. By "shock," Russell presumably meant offend the spirit of cooperation to which the paper and its readers were committed.

Eveline's moral paralysis at the end of the story seems to be brought
on in part by dedication to the family community. In Joyce's hands, that
devotion becomes decidedly evil. Eveline's decision to stay is no decision
at all; the dust of Dublin that surrounds and invades her body prevents
her leaving. And if the symbolism of the dust, reminiscent of the Ash
Wednesday reproach—"unto dust thou shalt return"—is not a strong
enough link between Dublin and death, the magnetic power of the dead
mother over Eveline's will makes the connection unmistakable. Here, for
the first time, we see Joyce using the ghost mother to represent the emotional blackmailer threatening the child who would leave home. Ireland
herself becomes that blackmailer for Joyce, who, like other emigrants,
continues to pay, in the form of his fiction, the price of escape.

"Eveline" was written near the anniversary of Mary Joyce's death.
Since that death, Joyce's sister Margaret had been keeping her promise

to her dying mother to look after the remaining children. Like Eveline, Margaret was often reduced to "wheedling shillings from her father," and often got verbally abused for her trouble (Ellmann, *James Joyce* 143). Joyce thus had a partial model for Eveline and her situation close at hand. What is interesting is the way in which Joyce ties that situation to the predicament of the would-be emigrant (who happened to be Joyce himself at the time "Eveline" was written).

Joyce implies that Eveline's promise to her mother, and everyone who participates in it, is to some extent evil. The mother, knowing the miserable quality of her own existence, is evil to ask that her daughter assume a similar existence and thereby forfeit her own identity; Eveline is evil because she is too scrupulous and too cowardly to cut herself away from the family and live a productive life with Frank. The promise "to keep the home together as long as she could" (*D* 40), a pledge conventionally interpreted as an admirable commitment to self-sacrifice for the sake of the family, becomes immoral by Joyce's manipulation. The promise is the sign of an improperly functioning conscience. Granting or refusing to grant a promise to one's dying mother contributes to a more and more complex theme in Joyce's works. That theme is always related to the conflict between individuality and communality, a conflict necessarily operative for the emigrant.

"The Sisters" and "Eveline" can serve to demonstrate the major thrust of the entire cycle of *Dubliners*. Joyce's Dubliner is a spiritually famished prisoner serving time in a barren cell to which there seems to be no key. Or, like Mr. Duffy, he is an "outcast from life's feast" (*D* 117), dying of starvation on a decaying island. Father Flynn's stupefying paralysis is reproduced in Eveline's passive helplessness, in Little Chandler's melancholy, dull resentment, and finally, in Gabriel Conroy's swooning soul.

In his "Conclusion" to *Contemporary Ireland,* Paul-Dubois repeats that "Ireland is at a turning point in her history. Her future—final decay or regeneration—depends on the direction she takes and the effort she puts forth. ... Either a new national Ireland arising with a soul remade, with recovered strength, and faculties of action reorganised, will take her place among the nations ... or the process of a final and fatal decay, making of the *Ile Verte* a dead and empty land ... will issue in the proscription and death of the Celtic race, who will thenceforth be condemned, like the Jews, to wander the world in an eternal exile" (512). In these closing comments, Paul-Dubois appeals to the fear of national extinction which had been aroused by the Famine and intensified by the resulting interminable emigration. It is this fear that partly accounts for the tendency among Irish emigrants such as Joyce to show cause for deserting the *Ile Verte*.

In *Portrait*, Joyce continues the defense, begun in the critical writings and *Dubliners*, of his decision to leave Ireland. As he had in *Stephen Hero*, he insists that individual integrity must precede national survival, and he depicts the Church as the dominant threat to that integrity. Significantly, integrity as represented in *Stephen Hero* and *Portrait* has a decidedly sexual component, so that sexuality and the Church's repressive power become enmeshed. Achieving sexual wholeness and wholesomeness is at least as important to Stephen as are his intellectual and artistic pursuits; indeed, there are sections in *Portrait* where sexual self-fashioning takes precedence over all other concerns.

In chapter 3, as Stephen's adolescent sexual drives begin pursuing him in the form of "intangible phantoms," he hears

> the constant voices of his father and of his masters, urging him to be a gentleman . . . and urging him to be a good catholic. These voices had now come to be hollowsounding in his ears . . . and when the movement towards national revival had begun to be felt in the college yet another voice had bidden him to be true to his country and help to raise up her fallen language and tradition. . . . And it was the din of all these hollowsounding voices that made him halt irresolutely in the pursuit of phantoms. He gave them ear only for a time but he was happy only when he was far from them, beyond their call, alone or in the company of phantasmal comrades. (*P* 83–84)

Earlier in the chapter we have learned that the phantasmal comrades haunting Stephen's reveries, who now supersede national and religious interests, are variations of Mercedes, "the unsubstantial image which his soul so constantly beheld" (*P* 65). That image is given substance by "E. C.," and at the end of the chapter the phantom takes the shape of a whore.

Stephen's sexual indulgences alone and with whores and his exaggerated guilt and fear-engendered repentance for his sins occupy the whole of chapter 3. The sexual–religious conflict depicted in this chapter is arguably the central "message" of the book. The message is that the methods used by the Church to shape the consciences of its young members are deceptive—apparently humane but actually contemptuous of humanity, especially of the normal sexual needs of young people. Following the retreat, which has left Stephen exhausted, aching, and chilled, he closes himself in his room "to be alone with his soul, to examine his conscience, to meet his [sexual] sins face to face, to recall their times and manners and circumstances, to weep over them" (P 139).

Attempts to form Stephen's conscience begin in the opening pages of the book, when Stephen's mother announces that "Stephen will apologise" (P 8), and continue through the pandying by Father Dolan, the beating by Heron and Boland, and Cranly's attacks "on the score of love for one's mother" (P 247). Most often the confrontations involve a type of confession. Always they represent a conflict between Stephen and some convention that he believes is particularly characteristic of Irish society: undue respect for priests and Catholicism, preferences for mediocre literature, overly strong attachments of Irish boys to their mothers (or vice versa), or, most important, an implicit abhorrence of healthy sexual appetites. By showing us how cultural pressures tend to mis-form the conscience of one young man in Ireland, Joyce shows us how the conscience of the nation has been mis-formed. As chapter 3 makes clear, the Church is ultimately responsible for all the false consciences, because it is the Church that instills false values.

After the retreat and his emotional confession to the unknown Capuchin, Stephen begins to live a scrupulously virtuous life. He finds, however, that "to merge his life in the common tide of other lives was harder for him than any fasting and prayer, and it was his constant failure to do this to his own satisfaction which caused in his soul at last a spiritual dryness together with a growth of doubts and scruples" (P 151–52).

In a letter to Nora dated August 29, 1904, Joyce explained that he had found it impossible to remain in the Catholic Church "on account of the impulses of [his] nature." Those impulses, we learn, are sexual. In the same letter he attempted to clear up a misunderstanding with Nora about what appears to have been a sexual encounter: "It was a sacrament which left in me a final sense of sorrow and degradation—sorrow because I saw in you an extraordinary, melancholy tenderness which had chosen that sacrament as a compromise, and degradation because I understood that in your eyes I was inferior to a convention in our present society" (L 2, 48, 49).

On September 16, 1904, Joyce wrote Nora, "It seemed to me that I was fighting a battle with every religious and social force in Ireland for you and that I had nothing to rely on but myself. There is no life here—

no naturalness or honesty" (*L 2*, 53). In 1905, Joyce justified his emigration in a letter to Stanislaus by claiming his "intention of living in conformity with [his] moral nature" (*L 2*, 99); living in conformity with his nature included living in a sexual relationship that had not been sanctioned by church or state. Joyce had to leave Ireland to be true to his sexual nature. He therefore linked sexual freedom in his own life, as he would have Stephen do in *Portrait*, with his urge to emigrate.

By the time *Portrait* was published in serial form in 1914, Freud had given the subject of sexuality a currency affecting every sort of text. In *Studies in the Psychology of Sex*, Havelock Ellis, too, had put the rhetoric of sexuality into circulation as never before. The writings of both men authorized a release from cultural and religious taboos and promised a resulting gain in self-control. Stephen Dedalus might be considered a paradigm of Western culture's transition from sexual repression to liberation. His vision of the bird-girl in many ways anticipates Foucault's definition of the deployment of sexuality: a discourse "in which sex, the revelation of truth, the overturning of global laws, the proclamation of a new day to come and the promise of a certain felicity are linked together" (*History of Sexuality* 7).

The bird-girl, a composite of sexual and religious symbolism, reveals to Stephen the essential goodness of sexuality. After Stephen's first "outburst of profane joy"

> Her image had passed into his soul for ever and no word had broken the holy silence of his ecstasy. Her eyes had called him and his soul had leaped at the call. To live, to err, to fall, to triumph, to recreate life out of life! . . . His soul was swooning into some new world, fantastic, dim, uncertain as under sea, traversed by cloudy shapes and beings. (*P* 172)

Joyce has been telling us in *Portrait* that the conscience of Stephen's race is uncreated because the Church has fooled the Irish into thinking that they have a properly functioning moral faculty, in effect substituting a false conscience for the real thing, particularly with regard to sexual matters. At the end of *Portrait*, finally having been able to see through the Church's distorted images of virtue, Stephen is prepared to begin devising icons of his own design, in the image of the bird-girl, for the moral edification of Ireland.

The road to Stephen's bird-girl had been arduous and haunted by dragons of guilt. After falling under her rejuvenating spell, however,

Stephen discovers that although the bird-girl has changed him, she has not changed Ireland. Ireland is still hopelessly contaminated by a religion that saps all of its vitality like a plague. Stephen has to leave the country, as Joyce convinced himself that he had to, lest the health and integrity of his new soul be threatened.

Richard Brown sees in Joyce's abandonment of the Church "a shift from belief in God to a belief in the sexual instincts that make up the human spirit" (126). If we accept that Joyce made such a shift, his works might be viewed as the product of a form of population control that Foucault believes is far more subtle and inescapable than the influence of any single church or nation. "The deployment of sexuality," according to Foucault, "has its reason for being, not in reproducing itself, but in proliferating, innovating, annexing, creating, and penetrating bodies in an increasingly detailed way, and in controlling populations in an increasingly comprehensive way" (*History of Sexuality* 107).

The power Foucault assigns the current discourse on sexuality is not deployed from a center of authority like the Church, not imposed from above, but is exerted from every direction by an elusive normalizing tendency, an equalizer appearing under the guise of a liberator. It is to such elusive and indefinable power sources, Foucault believes, that we must look to discover the true implications of population control. To examine the influence of the economy or the Church in Ireland on emigration, for example, is not sufficient without examining the discourses, such as that on sexuality, that impinge on and sometimes override those influences. On the surface, Stephen's conviction that he had to leave Ireland in order to live according to his true nature seems to have developed *against* the distorting power of the Church, but below and above that surface pressure was the current of a powerful discourse which Stephen responded *to*. Foucault would have us look more closely at that discourse.

Just as the *Irish Homestead,* the textual environment of Joyce's first published work of fiction, includes rhetorical conventions pressuring the Irish to stay in Ireland, so the *Egoist,* the first home of *Portrait,* includes rhetorical pressure to make sexuality the focus of intellectual, spiritual, and physical fulfillment. A letter in the February 16, 1914, issue, referring to a previous article on "The Chastity of Women," hopes that the article will be "the first in a series about men and women and their sex relations [because] ignorance of sex-anatomy, lack of sex consideration, blindness to the psychology of sex-desire, sex-pleasure, and sex-satisfaction cause to-day more misery, illness and hatred than all other causes whatsoever, veneral disease included" (78). Although the correspondent's concern about sexual misunderstandings seems overwrought in view of the fact that Europe was on the brink of World War I, it exemplifies Foucault's thesis that the discourse on sexuality may be the most inscrutably diversionary tactic of our time. In fact, the letter quoted began a lively explicit debate in the pages of the *Egoist* about sexual practices which continued throughout 1914 as Europe was falling apart and every sort of freedom was being called into question. The original article on chastity had appeared on February 2, Joyce's birthday, along with the first installment of *Portrait*.

Foucault suggests that to analyze the progress of the deployment of sexuality, we trace it down to instances of its actual material functioning, the "micropractices" of power relations that focus on sex. Among such micropractices is that of confession, particularly the sacrament of penance as it evolved after the Council of Trent. A thorough and probing examination of conscience before each confession, such as the examination Stephen is represented as having made in *Portrait*, was prescribed by the Council. A marked emphasis on the legalistic nature of the sacrament developed, with the priest taking on the qualities of a judge hearing a case; absolution became the passing of the sentence.

Foucault points out that the mandate to confess sexual irregularities originating in spiritual authority has undergone a transformation during the past hundred years or so. The injunction is now a secular one, crossing legal, medical, and sociological boundaries. As the Church has deemphasized the need for private auricular confession of sexual aberrations, society has demanded to hear more and more about the sexual practices of its citizens. And oddly enough, individuals who would very likely have suffered great anxiety at the thought of confessing to a priest (as Stephen did) willingly describe their sexual practices to a lawyer, physician, or talk-show host.

Because *Portrait* includes a sacramental confession conducted according to the guidelines of the Council of Trent, and because the novel is itself a confession of a more modern, psychoanalytic type, it uniquely exemplifies the micropractice of confession in transition. In the process of transition, one form of power wielded by a central, identifiable authority gives way to another, amorphous one, exerting its pressure from all sides. The action of *Portrait* moves toward the sacrament of penance, then away from that spiritual unburdening to the disclosures Stephen makes to his friends in chapter 5 in an attempt to reveal his moral (read sexual) nature. Significantly, *Portrait,* one in a series of revelations about his own sexuality which Joyce made in letters to Nora as well as in his fiction, is also a confession for him.

When Stephen tests his friends to determine whether they can be more satisfactory confessors than the priest, i.e., more open to his un-conventional disclosures and more ready to approve his moral nature, he is disappointed. "Why did you tell me those things?" asks Davin (*P* 202), while Cranly replies to "Stephen's ardent wayward confessions" with "harsh comments [and] sudden intrusions of rude speech" (*P* 232). His friends' reactions are at least as judgmental as the Capuchin's were. The priest had listened attentively and asked the prescribed questions of Stephen, but then had implored Stephen, as he was bound to do, "to give up that sin [of masturbation or fornication]." Finally the priest had spo-ken the grave words of absolution, and raised his hand above Stephen "in token of forgiveness" (*P* 144–45). But it was not really forgiveness that Stephen wanted any more than it is forgiveness that the psychoan-alytic patient wants. Stephen wanted approval, and reassurance that his sexual proclivities were not evil.

Clearly, there was no confessor who could confirm Stephen's moral nature in Ireland, a country whose allegiance to the Church insured that uninhibited sexual activity outside marriage (and much of it inside mar-riage) would apparently always be considered sinful. Stephen, like Joyce, therefore gave up the sacrament of penance, the Church, and Ire-land (for a time), but Joyce did not give up confessing. Rather, he re-placed the priest with a new confessor, the international reading public, and he substituted open, written discussion of sexuality for private au-ricular confession of "sins of the flesh." Joyce and his canon have thus become a prototype of the participant in Foucault's history of sexuality. *Ulysses* and the *Wake* continue the participation in the discourse, but they reveal a consciousness of their own "predicament," both in the sense of "category" and "trying situation." While Joyce's later works demonstrate the influence of deployed sexuality, they also ironically admit that sexual liberation is another convention, as sexual repression was, and one which is much more difficult either to understand or to break through. That ironic awareness is not apparent in the early works.

3

The Cultural Mandate Reconsidered

"You say you're emancipated but, in my opinion, you haven't got beyond the first book of Genesis yet."
—Cranly to Stephen Dedalus, *SH* 185

When Joyce, Nora, and the two children returned to Trieste in 1919, almost penniless, the once lively harbor was nearly deserted. The war-wounded straggled back to reassemble their lives and Joyce and his family moved into an overcrowded flat with his sister and her family. Their reception was less than cordial. Stanislaus, only recently released from Katzenau, moved out of the flat when he heard of his brother's imminent return, making clear his intention to maintain the estrangement already established between them. The emigré branch of the Joyce family thus became regrouping and redefining itself as so many other families were forced to do in the aftermath of the war. In many ways, postwar Europe began a genesis, an attempt to repopulate and recivilize the world after a catastrophe more devastating than flood or famine. Under these conditions, Joyce began working on "Oxen of the Sun."

When Oscar Schwarz asked Joyce how he had spent the war years, Joyce responded disinterestedly, "Oh yes, I was told there was a war going on in Europe" (Ellmann, *James Joyce* 472). But "Oxen" (and later the *Wake*) belie Joyce's apparent indifference. Describing Joyce's emotional state while working on "Oxen," Ellmann reports that Joyce "was so possessed by his theme that he felt as though he were himself eating the oxen, as though they were everywhere. It was hard to sit down to a meal without having his stomach turn" (*James Joyce* 476). Given these visceral reactions to his own work, it is difficult to believe that Joyce's theme in "Oxen" can be reduced to either a celebration of human procreation or a condemnation of contraceptive sex, as various critics have argued.

53

Joyce's remarks about his work on "Oxen" parallel the reaction of Lloyd George to the war: "The thing is horrible," he said, "and beyond human nature to bear, and I feel I can't go on any longer with the bloody business" (Fussell 174). Harriet Shaw Weaver found reading "Oxen" like "being taken the rounds of hell," and on completing the episode, Joyce wrote to Frank Budgen that "the oxen of the bloody bleeding sun are finished" (Ellmann, *James Joyce* 476). Yet birth and birth control are clearly central to the episode, and Harriet Shaw Weaver's reaction notwithstanding, "Oxen" includes some of the funniest passages in all of *Ulysses*.

The complex demographic aberrations that were brought about or emphasized by the war may partially account for the intricate and nearly indecipherable theme of "Oxen," as well as for its frequent references to the books of Genesis and Malachai. The war dead, the sudden return of thousands of soldiers, the relocation of refugees, and the changing roles of wives and mothers in the workplace all transformed the face of Europe. Most European governments were ill-equipped to deal with the postwar chaos. The contradictory discourses about population problems generated during the interwar years rivalled and surpassed the debates produced by that earlier, more parochial nightmare of history, the Famine.

As the European trench war dragged to its conclusion, the Anglo-Irish guerrilla war, fired by the residual heat of the 1916 Easter Uprising, commenced. From early 1919 to July 1921, the "troubles," as the people euphemistically called the war, seriously embittered Anglo-Irish relations (McCartny 311). During and after the First World War and the Anglo-Irish conflicts, a number of interrelated movements served to underscore the paradox of a civilization which theoretically held life to be sacred, yet permitted the unprecedented slaughter of carefully selected male adults. By 1920, the birth control movement, social Darwinism, and the eugenics controversy had gained international notoriety and influence. Counterforces such as the Catholic church and the populationists responded. The world became an arena where neo-Malthusianism and the cultural mandate of Genesis ("increase and multiply") vied for dominance.

Each contender for the title of savior of the race paradoxically represented a "crime committed against fecundity" as Joyce described the idea behind "Oxen" (Ellmann, *James Joyce* 475). The "crime" of the episode has long been a subject of debate among critics. Often it is equated with birth control, and Joyce's condemnation of artificial contraception and various forms of sterility is argued. In his study of Joyce and sexuality, Richard Brown provides an excellent resumé of critical opinion about the crime at the heart of "Oxen." Brown describes Joyce's purpose as "to give us a strong taste of militantly and rather oppressively 'reproductive' doctrines and show sympathetic characters like Bloom and Mina Purefoy on the receiving end of such views" (78).

Here Brown suggests that the doctrines about reproduction are criminals relentlessly imposing on individual procreative activity. I would expand Brown's implicit definition of the crime against fecundity to include socially sanctioned behavior (like war) that destroys lives and individual freedom in the name of preserving political, religious, or ethnic institutions. Joyce further explained the idea behind "Oxen" as "sterilizing the act of coition" (Ellmann, *James Joyce* 475). On a large scale, the wars ending and beginning in Joyce's world frustrated or counteracted the reproductive function of coition. And, more and more militantly, the ideologies marking the birth control movement, social Darwinism, and eugenics policed the act of coition by justifying and vigorously encouraging the sterilization of individual acts, creating pressures to control the size, quality, and ethnic makeup of a population, and ultimately developing rhetorical conventions that would lead to another world war.

Like the rest of *Ulysses*, the fictional "Oxen" occurs on June 16, 1904, when neither Ireland nor the world was at war. But no fiction is created in a temporal or cultural vacuum, and the various forms of population control prevalent in 1919 all participate in the slaughter of Joyce's oxen. "What, says Mr Leopold," speaking of the diseased cattle, "will they slaughter all?" (*U* 399.12–14: *U* 14.565–67). Not only Bloom and Mina Purefoy, but all of the characters in the episode are victims of the slaughter, because their freedom to proliferate is limited by economic, ethnic, nationalistic, or religious sanctions of which they are often unaware. It is in this sense of limiting procreative behavior for ideological ends that I believe Joyce meant "sterilizing the act of coition." The narrator (and occasionally Stephen and Bloom) seems to be ironically aware of the crime in progress, and indeed may represent the voice of Western civilization that is perpetrating the crime.

The various representatives of population control speak both directly and indirectly in "Oxen." Often, just as the rhetoric of the Famine seems to be lifted from other texts and incorporated into Joyce's works, so "Oxen" is filled with the rhetoric of population control current in the texts of early twentieth-century Europe. The crime of the episode is established in the opening two paragraphs where fecundity is at first unabashedly celebrated, but finally is called into question. From the joyful prayer for "quickening and wombfruit," the prelude to "Oxen" moves into a disputation of the cultural mandate of Genesis, "that evangel simultaneously command and promise which on all mortals with prophecy of abundance or with diminution's menace that exalted of reiteratedly procreating function ever irrevocably enjoined" (*U* 383.33–37: *U* 14.29–32).

The prelude to "Oxen" signifies the hopeless struggle of the individual to understand and comply with the dictates of population. The elements in the problem of population control are intermixed and superimposed on one another so that the very real frustration experienced in trying to solve that problem is conveyed to the reader. Some of the rhetorical conventions (or parodies of conventions) used in the prelude are: "general consent"; "the prosperity of a nation"; "proliferant continuance"; "a downwardtending lutulent [i.e., muddy] reality"; "no nature's boon can contend against the bounty of increase"; "every most just citizen [should] become the exhortator and admonisher of his semblables" (i.e., fellowmen); "what had in the past been by the nation excellently commenced might be in the future not with similar excellence accomplished." The arguments of political economists, fundamentalists, Malthusians, neo-Malthusians, eugenicists, and individualists are all brought to rest, founded, on the cultural mandate of Genesis.

The war enters the prelude, and indeed the whole of "Oxen," primarily by way of its ironic mode. In *The Great War and Modern Memory*, Paul Fussell demonstrates how the passage of modern writing from the realistic to the ironic mode parallels the passage from "prewar freedom to wartime bondage, frustration, and absurdity" (312). The irony of the prelude arises from the contradiction between the apparent rationality of its appeal to the acumen of the "most just citizen" regarding birth control and the confusing, inscrutable message about how and when to exercise that control. What *is* clear is that some power other than the individual decides the appropriateness of procreative behavior and that that power constantly changes its shape and its priorities. The resulting situation for the individual is frustrating and absurd.

But the war also enters "Oxen" more directly. The narrator begins an indictment of Bloom's mild and unspoken reproval of the students' frivolity in the "puerperal dormitory" by referring back to the altercation between Bloom and the Citizen: "During the recent war whenever the enemy had a temporary advantage with his granados did this traitor to his kind not seize the moment to discharge his piece against the empire of which he is a tenant at will while he trembled for the security of his four per cents?" (*U* 409.8–13: *U* 14.909–12). This is the rhetoric of the patriot, Irish or otherwise, who cannot abide a dissenting view about the nation's right to be at war. The narrator ties this censorious attack on Bloom's good citizenship to Bloom's behavior in the bedchamber, which, we are led to believe, is contraceptive in nature, and therefore every bit as reprehensible as the behavior of the students. Bloom is, after all, a married man, and should be contributing good citizens to the community like that virile "old buckoo," Theodore Purefoy. However, Bloom's duty and ability to reproduce are undercut later in the passage when his foreign origins are again invoked as they had been in "Cyclops." Bloom is "at his best an exotic tree which, when rooted in its native orient, throve and flourished and was abundant in balm but, transplanted to a clime more temperate, its roots have lost their quondam vigour while the stuff that comes away from it is stagnant, acid and inoperative" (*U* 410.1–6: *U* 14.937–41).

The passage, beginning with the reference to the recent war and ending with the description of Bloom's sterility, incorporates numerous overlapping arguments used in various defenses of population control: the unquestionable right of the nation to make war and implicitly to send men off to be slaughtered; the duty of the married, employed citizen to reproduce and replace those lost men; the unsuitability of certain races to certain "climes." The passage gets progressively more despondent, a tone that is picked up and repeated several pages later in the "Agendath is a waste land" section (*U* 414.12–29: *U* 14.1086–1109).

Paul Fussell points out how common the wasteland and the Slough of Despond images are in the literature surrounding the Great War. "It would be impossible to count the number of times 'the Slough of Despond' is invoked as the only adequate designation for churned-up mud morasses [and also] 'the Valley of the Shadow of Death,' where, in Bunyan, 'lay blood, bones, ashes, and mangled bodies of men, even of Pilgrims that had gone this way formerly' " (139). Joyce employs this convention several times in *Ulysses*, most often connecting the wasteland image with Bloom. Thus Bloom comes to represent not only the pilgrim of the piece and Ulysses, the returning warrior, but also the impotent aging king invoked in the mythology of agrarian societies to account for the failure of fecundity.

The mysterious man in the mackintosh who appears in several places throughout *Ulysses* may also be a variation on a theme that originated in war lore. Fussell recounts the widely circulated tale of the phantom German officer-spy who appears in the British trenches just before an attack. No one sees him arrive or leave, he is never captured, and his mystery is never solved. He is described in Edmund Blunden's *Undertones of War:* "A stranger in a soft cap and a trench coat approached, and asked me the way to the German lines. This visitor facing the east was white-faced as a ghost, and I liked neither his soft cap nor his mackintosh nor the right hand concealed under the coat. . . . I thought he must be a spy" (quoted in Fussell 122). Joyce's man in the mackintosh first appears in "Hades," the complement of "Oxen," where Bloom wonders "who is that lankylooking galoot in the mackintosh?" Subsequently, Bloom realizes that the man in the mackintosh brings the number in the funeral party to thirteen, "death's number" (*U* 109.29–30, 110–11: *U* 6.805, 826). In the concluding pages of "Oxen," he appears as a once prosperous citizen, now the "Walking Mackintosh of Lonely Canyon" (*U* 427.24–25: *U* 14.1546–53). On one level his mackintosh is a contraceptive, as are most waterproofing devices in Joyce's works (see Bowen, "Joyce's Prophylactic Paralysis"). The man in the mackintosh has no identity outside of the rubber preservative he wears; he is a gigantic perambulating condom avoiding life's deluge. But as the logical conclusion, the end product, of the sterile, contraceptive society Bloom seems to fear, the man in the mackintosh might be Bloom's own doppelganger.

In addition to influencing the tone and the mythological underpinnings of "Oxen," war enters the episode by way of references such as "Jackjohn's bivouac" (*U* 394.31: *U* 14.407), "dispatches from the emperor's chief tailtickler" (*U* 399.23–24: *U* 14.574), "deliver yourself wholly into the hands of the enemy or . . . quit the field" (*U* 404.39–40: *U* 14.761), and the "granados" in the passage quoted above. And, of course, the slaughter of the cattle can be taken to represent the sacrificial slaughter of soldiers in every war.

The emphasis in "Oxen" on artificial contraceptives can be attributed to the pressures of the birth control movement that was sweeping pre- and postwar Europe and the United States. Although that movement became associated with Malthus in the mind of the public, its philosophy had actually undergone numerous transformations prior to 1919. Malthus had asserted that when unchecked by "natural restraints" such as famine, for example, population increases in a geometric ratio while food supplies increase arithmetically. As the prelude to "Oxen" would have it, "no nature's boon can contend against the bounty of increase." To bring the two forces into balance, Malthus advocated "moral restraint" among married couples.

Francis Place, one of the earliest public advocates of artificial contraceptives, retained Malthus's economic argument in favor of restraint, but considerably modified the argument about means. To expect young married couples, or young people generally, to remain celibate was un-reasonable and unrealistic, Place argued, yet unlimited progeny led to poverty and misery; therefore, a solution had to be found which would allow (in the words of "Oxens' " parody of Carlyle) "copulation without population" (*U* 423.38–39: *U* 14.1422). Place published his *Illustrations and Proofs of the Principle of Population* in 1822. In that work, "Place crystallized the latent longings of men and women into a social movement that had as its sole commitment separating the sexual appetite from the desire for progeny" (Chandrasekhar 19). Obviously, Place did not originate the desire for sexual intercourse without the fear of offspring; rather, he made it seem a civic duty to indulge that desire. Richard Brown has discovered that Place's pamphlet was advertised in *Photo Bits*, and Brown suggests that the "useful hints for marrieds" referred to in "Circe" may be an allusion to Place's *Illustrations and Proofs* (66).

Eventually the influence of Place's doctrines surfaced in Charles Knowlton's *Fruits of Philosophy*, the "corpus delecti of the Bradlaugh–Besant Trial" of 1877–1878 (Chandrasekhar 19). Although the pamphlet caused public outrage, there was a countercurrent of approval of Knowlton's work. As S. Chandrasekhar points out, "this was a remarkable turning point, for until this moment no regular newspaper would touch the subject [of artificial contraception], much less endorse it" (42). Because Knowlton was a doctor, the use of contraceptives and the birth control movement acquired a dimension of legitimacy which Place, a laborer, had been unable to convey. A passage from the "Philosophical Proem" introducing Knowlton's subject demonstrates how the cultural mandate had been appropriated and transformed by *The Fruits of Philosophy*. Knowlton observes that

> man by nature is endowed with the talent of devising means to remedy or prevent the evils that are liable to arise from gratifying our appetites; and it is as much the duty of the physician to inform mankind of the means of preventing the evils that are liable to arise from gratifying the reproductive instinct, as it is to inform them how to keep clear of the gout or the dyspepsia (quoted in Chandrasekhar 97).

Early in "Oxen," where the narrator is ostensibly praising the devotion of Irish doctors to the art of healing, the narrator slips into the passage the equivocal phrase "whereby maternity was from all accident possibility removed" (*U* 384.12–13: *U* 14.45–46). Eliminating the element of chance from motherhood was precisely what Knowlton and the neo-Malthusians hoped to do. Given the sanction of medicine, a branch of science, birth control became simply another way of carrying out the cultural mandate. Joyce picks up on the irony of the physician as birth controller early in "Oxen" and exploits that irony throughout the episode.

Knowlton's remarks invite another ironic reading with important implications for *Ulysses*. Knowlton implicitly equates the "reproductive instinct" with the urge for sexual intercourse, thus implying that if the urge for sexual relief is fulfilled, the reproductive instinct is satisfied. Joyce seems to question that equation in the person of Leopold Bloom. For example, in spite of the fact that Bloom has just "relieved" himself sexually in "Nausicaa," his reproductive instinct remains unsatisfied, and, like the aging king, he is unable to rejuvenate his wasteland kingdom.

The Bradlaugh–Besant trial of 1876, in which Annie Besant and Charles Bradlaugh were tried for publishing Charles Knowlton's *Fruits of Philosophy*, gave the birth control movement, spearheaded by "neo-Malthusians," its greatest impetus. During Joyce's lifetime, the neo-Malthusians actively promulgated the doctrine of Malthus according to Place as legitimized by Knowlton in thousands of lectures, pamphlets, and a journal, *The Malthusian* (published in London, 1879–1921). Bradlaugh and Besant clearly stated their purpose and their debt to Malthus in their "Publishers' Preface" to *Fruits of Philosophy:* "We believe, with the Rev. Mr. Malthus, that population has a tendency to increase faster than means of existence, and that *some* checks must therefore exercise control over population. . . . The checks that ought to control population are scientific, and it is these which we advocate" (quoted in Chandrasekhar 91). It is primarily to this corrupted version of Malthusianism that "Oxen" responds.

The inspiration for articulating the texts of Genesis and neo-Malthusianism, as Joyce does in "Oxen," seems to have come naturally to him. His professed love of the Bible (Ellmann, *James Joyce* 218) implies his love of Genesis. Furthermore, in a letter written to his father in 1922, Joyce mentions that the Bible is "a book which like *Ulysses*, no good Catholic should read" (Ellmann, *James Joyce* 540). No doubt, Joyce intended a number of analogies between *Ulysses* and the Bible, one of which might have been the frankness of the two books regarding sexual matters. Such plain language, in Joyce's view, would be particularly offensive to the "carnophobic" sensibilities of Catholics, as would the frank discussions of contraceptive devices and sexual activities in the pamphlets distributed by birth control advocates. Implicit in Joyce's comparison of *Ulysses* to the Bible, too, is his belief in the universality and comprehensiveness of the theme of his work.

Like his interest in the Bible, Joyce's interest in contraceptive practices was long-standing. Zack Bowen points out that the paralysis theme pervasive in *Dubliners* is often linked to a prophylactic motif: "The characters in these stories have sought to cloak themselves from exposure to weather, sex, and emotion in insulation. Like its prophylactic counterpart, the covering severely limits sensation, pleasure, and the creative force" ("Joyce's Prophylactic Paralysis" 259). Bowen argues that the various waterproofing devices, "particularly hats, waterproofs, and umbrellas," symbolize their owners' attempts "to cloak their exposure to the vicissitudes of church- and state-dominated morality" (259). Bowen's thesis is substantiated in "Oxen," where contraceptive practices become tropes for every sort of barrier to human productivity and communication, whether intellectual, spiritual, emotional, or physical. Thus, for example, Lenehan's ability to "bring himself off with his tongue" conflates a contraceptive practice with Lenehan's prevaricating, fraudulent nature (*U* 398.26–27: *U* 14.542–43).

In "Oxen"—as in *Dubliners,* where Michael Furey risks death by serenading Gretta in the rain—water and wetting are symbolic of courage, creativity, and, paradoxically, of death. But death by water is a *vital* death; like the discharge of amniotic fluid which heralds the termination of a pregnancy and an imminent birth, rain and wetting symbolize both end and beginning. In Genesis, too, the flood is a paradoxical symbol of both the end and the beginning of civilization. Although new life for the world and a second chance at establishing the perfect society are promised to Noah and his offspring, all the conflicts implied in the cultural mandate given Adam and Eve are subsequently imposed on Noah's progeny. In Joyce's lifetime, those conflicts were reimposed on postwar Western civilization as well.

In what is arguably the most ingenious use of a contraceptive trope in all of "Oxen," Joyce implicitly turns Noah's ark into a condom and the water of the flood into a deluge of semen. During a discussion about the relative merits of various types of contraceptive devices, Lynch poohpoohs the value of the "cloak" (condom), in favor of the "umbrella" (diaphragm); he points out that his "dear Kitty . . . would dance in a deluge before ever she would starve in such an ark of salvation" (*U* 405.28–30: *U* 14.787–88). If this analogy is stretched to its limit, Noah becomes a moral coward who escaped the revivifying force of the flood by using an artificial (for the ark is a product of Noah's artifice) preservative. The passage also reflects an actual controversy in progress within the birth control movement about the relative merits of condoms and diaphragms.

Brown points out that Joyce read both religious and secular material on the subject of contraceptives. He owned works presenting the traditional teachings of the Church, such as Paul Garnier's *Onanisme* and M. M. Matharan's *Causus de Matrimonio fere quingenti*, and seems to have read Havelock Ellis's the *New Spirit* and *Studies in the Psychology of Sex*, which provide secular, eugenicist views. Between the extremes of viewpoint on contraception represented by these texts, there were the socialist discussions of the subject found in the preface to Shaw's *Getting Married* and Fabian tracts on "The Decline in the Birth-Rate" and "Francis Place." W. E. H. Lecky's the *History of European Morals*, also in Joyce's library, presents the unfolding of Christian attitudes toward sexuality from the point of view of a social Darwinist. Additionally, magazines like *Photo Bits* (the source of the Blooms' bedroom picture, "The Bath of the Nymph") were "common popular sources for contraceptive information" (Brown 66). In "Some Points on Poyntz and Related Matters," James F. Carens demonstrates the likelihood that the Poyntz hosiers in Dublin, to whom Joyce alludes in "Oxen," trafficked in illegal contraceptives. The influences of all of these sources are found in "Oxen" and elsewhere in *Ulysses*, but Brown makes an important point about the way these influences are felt in Joyce's texts: "Birth and birth-control issues were not ones which Joyce used only as structuring devices, or even primarily as the basis of an analogy for artistic process. They emerge as motivating issues ... the effect of Joyce's method being at once to respond to the contentiousness of the issues as felt by Catholics and to offer his contribution in a language which ... filters [the reader's] attention through a variety of past formulations and attitudes" (77).

Garnier's *Onanisme*, published in 1885, reflected Catholic tradition and therefore condemned all forms of non-reproductive sexual activity. Brown notes that Garnier writes against "all artificial obstacles to human generation," including not only specifically contraceptive practices, but also sexual perversities (55). Matharan, too, provides a casuistical history of the Church's teachings on birth control as part of his treatise on marriage. Brown suggests that Matharan may have been the source for Joyce's references to *emissio seminis inter vas naturale* in *Exiles* (*E* 173) and *Ulysses* (*U* 223.31: *U* 10.168). Adaline Glasheen identifies Matharan as the source for the Honuphrius section of the Porter chapter of the *Wake* (129); like "Oxen," that episode—which will be discussed in some detail in the next chapter—examines the impact of a contraceptive philosophy on the lives of individuals.

It seems likely that the very "idea" of "Oxen" derives from the rhetoric of the Church doctors. Ever since Augustine's *Marriage and Concupiscence* in the fourth century, the Church fathers have referred to contraceptives as "poisons of sterility" frustrating the procreative function of sexual intercourse (see Noonan, *Contraception* 136). The setting of "Oxen" may also have been determined by Joyce's reading of the Church fathers on birth control. In his history of contraception as treated by Catholic theologians, John T. Noonan records that St. John Chrysostom turned his attention to the subjects of prostitution and contraception:

> Why do you sow where the field is eager to destroy the fruit? Where there are medecines of sterility? Where there is murder before birth? You do not even let a harlot remain only a harlot, but you make her a murderess as well. ... from drunkenness comes fornication, from fornication adultery, from adultery ... something worse than murder ... for she does not kill what is formed but prevents its formation. What then? ... Do you make the *anteroom of birth* the *anteroom of slaughter*? (quoted in Noonan, *Contraception* 98; emphasis mine)

The analogy Chrysostom makes between the vagina and the anteroom of birth is suggested in "Oxen," where the hospital represents the womb (Ellmann, *James Joyce* 475), and the drunken students have turned its anteroom into the scene of the linguistic slaughter of innocence. On two separate occasions the narrator refers to the waiting room as an antechamber. Following the passage where Mulligan outlines his plan for a "fertilising farm," the fun ends with "some larum in the antechamber" (*U* 404.9–10: *U* 14.736–77).

Again, at the end of Bloom's reverie about his first meeting with Stephen, and just before the departure of the company for Burke's pub, the inscrutable narrator cautions the reader "to mark this further and remember. The end comes suddenly. Enter that antechamber of birth where the studious are assembled and note their faces" (*U* 422.29–31: *U* 14.1379–80). The epic simile that follows likens the sudden transformation of the vigilant students into a disorganized mob to the coming of the flood. Another echo of Chrysostom's homily is heard in Bloom's regretful suspicion that Stephen "lived riotously with those wastrels and murdered his goods with whores" (*U* 391.1–2: *U* 14.275–76). Here the whores, like Chrysostom's harlots, are implicated in the crime of murder just as Stephen is.

If Joyce did not actually read Chrysostom's homily, he may have heard passages from it repeated in sermons, such as those of Bernard Vaughan. In her chapter on the sermon as "Massproduct," Cheryl Herr demonstrates the pervasive influence of sermons on the thinking of the Irish people, noting particularly the persistence of the impression Vaughan made on Joyce. Joyce mentions Vaughan in three of his works of fiction, and in a letter to Stanislaus, speaking of the *Sinn Fein* campaign against "venereal excess," Joyce asserts that "if I put down a bucket into my own soul's well, sexual department, I draw up Griffith's and Ibsen's and Skeffington's and Bernard Vaughan's . . . along with my own. And I am going to do that in my novel. . . . I am nauseated by their lying drivel about pure men and pure women and spiritual love and love forever: blatant lying in the face of the truth" (quoted in Herr 229–30).

Joyce wrote that letter in 1906 when, as I see it, he was still determined to invoke the Church's restrictive attitude toward sexuality to defend his decision to leave Ireland. In *Ulysses*, however, the attitude toward sexuality has become more complex and Joyce uses Chrysostom's theology to set up his own treatment of population control as much to demonstrate the elusiveness of the truth about sexual matters as to point up the Church's excessive emphasis on chastity. At any rate, the letter suggests that venereal excesses were openly discussed in all forms of media, including sermons, in the first decade of the century. Sidney Webb's socialist tract on "The Decline in the Birth-Rate" corroborates that suggestion.

The number and variety of probable debts to W. E. H. Lecky's *History of European Morals* in "Oxen" is marked. For example, Lecky's treatment of the influence of Christianity on eliminating the customs of infanticide and abortion (24–25) is echoed in both "Hades" and "Oxen of the Sun." Significantly, Lecky's work conveys an attitude as well as facts about the history of European morals. Praising "the enlightened charity of Malthus," Lecky especially compliments Malthus's economically sound design for the practice of Christian charity as opposed to the practices of the Catholic Church:

> In all Catholic countries where ecclesiastical influences have been permitted to develop unmolested, the monastic organisations have proved a deadly canker, corroding *the prosperity of the nation*. With-

drawing multitudes from all production, encouraging a blind and pernicious almsgiving, diffusing habits of improvidence ... fostering an ignorant admiration for saintly poverty, and an equally ignorant antipathy to the *habits and aims of an industrial civilisation,* they have *paralysed all energy* and proved an insuperable barrier to *material progress.* (100; emphasis mine)

Although Lecky does not mention Ireland specifically in this diatribe, Ireland is clearly the country he has primarily in mind. Since he was himself Irish and a Dubliner, it seems safe to say that Ireland is the Catholic country he knew best. The attitude expressed about the pernicious ecclesiastical influences on the laity is quite close to Plunkett's point of view in his *Ireland in the New Century,* but the use of Malthus to chastise the Church for its false notion of charity is new. Interestingly, Lecky uses the paralysis metaphor as Joyce does, to characterize the effect of the Church's power over the people.

Lecky's argument can be reduced to the premise that charity should be determined by political economy, or as it is often called, "the prosperity of the nation." This argument, used by England to defend its responses to Ireland's plight during the Famine, also appears in Bradlaugh and Besant, who plead "the nation's welfare" as justification for publishing Knowlton's instructions on birth control. The socialist, anti-neo-Malthusian, Sidney Webb (in a pamphlet Joyce owned) invokes the same cause. The anti-charity argument would also be used by eugenicists to deplore the proliferation of the poorer, weaker classes. In "Oxen" Joyce does not respond directly to Lecky's case against Catholic misinterpretation of charity, but reflects on the perniciousness of a philosophy that restricts human freedom to only those behaviors that enhance the nation's or church's welfare. Embedded in the prelude is his ironic commentary on sacrificing the human will to the prosperity of the nation.

Lecky's influence is felt again in "Oxen" in the section on one of Joyce's favorite subjects—confession. In the play on Irish, English, and papal bulls, Joyce's lifelong interest (obsession might not be too strong a word) in the power of the confessional combines with the subject of contraception. Cheryl Herr notes that Joyce's "general enhancement of titillating discourse [in confession] recalls the argument of Michel Foucault in *The History of Sexuality* that after the Council of Trent the Roman Catholic church extended its power through the ritual of confession [encouraging] the penitent's discourse on his or her sexual desires and actions" (267). Joyce had anticipated Foucault in his comment to Ettore Schmitz about psychoanalysis: "Well, if we need it, let us keep to confession" (quoted in Ellmann, *James Joyce* 472). As I have noted in the previous chapter, Joyce both keeps to confession and transforms it into a literary type of psychoanalysis; in "Oxen," he will refashion it into a contraceptive device.

The bull-session section of "Oxen" (*U* 399.30–401.26: *U* 14.573–650) makes the Church responsible for the emigration of Irish men. Underlying their decision to leave is the fact that the women, satisfied with the titillation of confession, lose interest in real, productive sexual intercourse: "So that maid, wife, abbess and widow to this day affirm that they would rather any time of the month whisper in his ear in the dark of a cowhouse or get a lick on the nape from his long holy tongue than lie with the finest strapping young ravisher in the four fields of all Ireland" (*U* 400.6–10: *U* 14.595–99). The confessional thus becomes an artificial contraceptive in two ways: it substitutes an unproductive type of intercourse for a productive one; and it forces the "seeds" of Ireland to be spilt on foreign ground.

It is tempting to argue that Joyce, either simply to get a laugh or to fortify his case against the authority of the Church, overstates the case for the power of confession. But all the implications of Joyce's burlesques are made with serious intent in Lecky's history, where Foucault's theory—that the seeds for sexual deployment were planted several centuries ago by institutions like the Church itself—is anticipated.

Describing the influence of St. Francis of Assisi over St. Clare, Lecky reveals the source of the Church's power over the faithful:

> The first nun, whom St. Francis of Assisi enrolled . . . was a beautiful girl of Assisi, named Clara Scifi, with whom he had for some time carried on a clandestine correspondence, and whose flight from her father's home he both counselled and planned. As the first enthusiasm of asceticism died away, what was lost in influence by the father was gained by the priest. The confessional made this personage the confidant in the most delicate secrets of domestic life. The supremacy of authority, of sympathy, and sometimes even of affection, passed away beyond the domestic circle, and by establishing an absolute authority over the most secret thoughts of nervous and credulous women, the priests laid the foundation of the empire of the world. (144)

Lecky implies that access to sexual secrets gave the priests power to rule the world, to control populations. Foucault carries that implication several steps further in his *History of Sexuality*, demonstrating that the discourse on sexuality itself has wrested power from the priests and is now to some extent controlling Western civilization. Joyce's works seem both to concur with Lecky's assessment and, to a limited extent, to exemplify Foucault's.

Although Joyce apparently resented the Church's influence over the sexual responses of its female members, his Catholic upbringing seems to have indelibly marked his attitude toward birth control. On one hand, he knew from experience the strain of surviving in a large, poor family, and it would therefore seem that he would have embraced the doctrines of the neo-Malthusians. On the other hand, Joyce's expressed attitudes imply that despite some of his otherwise freethinking views (toward marriage, for example), he saw the matter of birth control from a turn-of-the-century Catholic perspective. That perspective had been seriously challenged by the birth controllers and the eugenicists, to whom the Church reacted in the early years of the century by emphasizing the sacredness of *all* human life and reaffirming the Old Testament belief that children are a sign of God's bounty. To some extent, the Church even began to devalue celibacy (see chapter 13 in Noonan, *Contraception*).

In his Paris notebook Joyce quoted from Aristotle: "The most natural act for living beings which are complete is to produce other beings like themselves and thereby to participate as far as they may in the eternal and divine." In 1905 he told his sister Eva, "The most important thing that can happen to a man is the birth of a child." And many years later Joyce said to Louis Gillet, "I can't understand households without children. I see some with dogs, gimcracks. Why are they alive? To leave nothing behind, not to survive yourself—how sad!" (quoted in Ellmann, *James Joyce* 204). Furthermore, Bonnie Kime Scott reports that in a conversation with Sylvia Beach, Joyce regretted "that he didn't have ten children" (*Joyce and Feminism* 105). There are no signs of the prudent neo-Malthusian in Joyce's expressed attitude. Children seem unrelated to economic issues in these remarks. Nonetheless, after Nora's miscarriage in 1908, she and Joyce apparently chose not to have any more children.

In contrast to the positive view of fatherhood reflected in the statements quoted above, Joyce's painful awareness of the combined effect of poverty and overreproduction on his own family is made clear in a 1904 letter to Nora:

> My home was simply a middle-class affair ruined by spendthrift habits which I have inherited. My mother was slowly killed, I think, by my father's ill-treatment, by years of trouble, and by my cynical frankness of conduct. When I looked on her face as she lay in her

coffin—a face grey and wasted with cancer—I understood that I
was looking on the face of a victim and I cursed the system which
had made her a victim. We were seventeen in family. My brothers
and sisters are nothing to me. One brother alone is capable of understanding me. (quoted in Ellmann, *James Joyce* 169)

The conflicts implicit in Joyce's expressed attitudes and his behavior
about birth control become incorporated in his fiction. For example, the
contrast between Bloom's mild censure of the overreproductive Dedalus
family in "Lestrygonians" and the Dickensian narrator's sentimental ap-
probation of the Purefoys in "Oxen" sends a mixed message about birth
control deriving both from the personal author of *Ulysses* and from the
text of Western culture.

The narrator of "Oxen" describes Purefoy: "He is older now ...
and a trifle stooped in the shoulders yet in the whirligig of years a grave
dignity has come to the conscientious second accountant of the Ulster
bank, College Green branch." A list of the Purefoy children follows,
many of whom are named after prominent citizens of the United Kingdom (in contrast to the Dedalus children, all of whom are named after
saints) including the newborn, who "will be christened Mortimer Edward after the influential third cousin of Mr. Purefoy in the Treasury
Remembrancer's office, Dublin Castle" (*U* 421.2–9: *U* 14.1334–35).
This is a family that—according to much socialist propaganda, such
as that of Lecky, Webb, and Shaw—clearly had a right, even a duty, to
multiply.

Heavily laced with traditional Catholic teaching on birth control,
"Oxen" is equally marked by the socialist and eugenicist attitudes expressed in the first decades of the century. In "The Decline in the Birth-
Rate," one of a set of bound Fabian tracts in Joyce's library, Sidney Webb
reports on a Fabian Society study made "to consider birth-rate and in-
fantile mortality statistics" in 1906 (2). Webb makes a case against birth
control—especially against contraceptive practices for "desirable" families (such as the Purefoys). In formulating his arguments, Webb recounts the recent history of conflicting attitudes to population control, a
history echoed in the prelude to "Oxen."

Webb first suggests that the aspirations of Malthus are being fulfilled, for there is a decline in the birthrate throughout Great Britain,
with the notable exception of Roman Catholic Ireland. "Among the Roman Catholics in the United Kingdom any regulation of the married

state is strongly forbidden ... both privately and from the pulpit" (9). Elsewhere, in an argument with *himself* about the right of the individual to practice birth control, Webb refers more obliquely to Catholicism: "Apart from some mystic idea of marriage as a 'sacrament,' or, at any rate, as a divinely instituted relation with peculiar religious obligations for which utilitarian reasons cannot be given, it does not seem easy to argue that prudent regulation differs essentially from deliberate celibacy from prudent motives" (36). After demonstrating the likelihood that the use of artificial contraceptives, outside of the Catholic community, is otherwise rampant among the thrifty and prudent throughout the Empire, Webb shows that overpopulation is not so much the problem as is underpopulation of the fittest. "This can hardly result in anything but national deterioration; or, as an alternative, in this country gradually falling to the Irish or the Jews" (17).

Besides a certain Deasyan anti-Semitism—"Mark my words, Mr. Dedalus, [Mr. Deasy] said. England is in the hands of the jews ... and they are signs of a nation's decay" (*U* 33.28–30: *U* 2.346–48)—Webb's remarks have several implications for Joyce's works. Joyce would have been exposed to the Church's propaganda against birth control, mentioned in Webb's tract, before he left Ireland, and no doubt would have viewed it as yet another abuse of power on the part of the Church. Nonetheless, Joyce would have also been sensitive to Webb's xenophobic implication that a proliferation of the Irish in the British Empire would be highly undesirable and threatening to the purity of the British race. Webb's tract clearly demonstrates the pervasiveness of ideological pressures to control the act of coition and the insidious forms those pressures often take.

Elsewhere in the tract, Webb points out that "the limitation of numbers, however prudent it may be in individual instances, is, from the national standpoint, seen to be economically as unnecessary as it is proved to be futile even for the purposes for which McCulloch and Mill, Cairnes and Fawcett so ardently desired it" (16). What develops from Webb's assessment of the population situation is a sense of the constantly fluctuating attitudes toward both quantity and quality of population and the interaction of religious and political discourses on the subject. Webb's consideration of the problem "from the national standpoint" and his suggestion that what was in the fairly recent past thought to be economically desirable (i.e., a declining birthrate) is now clearly not desirable are, again, analogous to the prelude of "Oxen."

Shaw's preface to *Getting Married*, another socialist "tract" that Joyce owned, declares that "marriage is now beginning to depopulate the country with . . . alarming rapidity. . . . the licentiousness of marriage, now that it no longer recruits the race, is destroying it" (189). Shaw used headlines in his preface in somewhat the same ironic fashion that Joyce uses them in "Aeolus." Under the heading "The Question of Population," Shaw summarizes the problem: "To maintain the population at its present figure, or to increase it, we must take immediate steps to induce people of moderate means to marry earlier and to have more children. There is less urgency in the case of the very poor and the very rich" (207).

Typically, Shaw makes a very sharp point. His precision and clarity about the desirability of selective population growth are refreshing compared to Webb's more "lutulent"—even though statistically substantiated—prejudices. Again, as it did in Webb's tract, the profile of the Purefoys materializes. Again, the "sacrament" of marriage comes under attack. In a two-page account of "Christian Marriage," Shaw gives a satirical history of the fickle teachings of the Church about the value of sexuality. First, the Church abolished sex; then, realizing that the world was not going to end any time soon, the Church reinstated sexual intercourse and transformed it into a sacred act to be indulged in only under license of the Church itself. Shaw's own bias becomes clear when he asserts that the "great natural purpose [of the sex act] completely transcends the personal interests of any individual or even any ten generations of individuals" (220). In "Oxen," Mulligan only half ironically calls sexual intercourse "the noblest task for which our bodily organism has been framed" (U 402.5–6: U 14.665). Shaw's and Mulligan's attitudes toward procreation are oddly both similar and contrary to Genesis. They imply that there is a cultural mandate transcending individual rights which determines the size and quality of the population, but neither Shaw nor Mulligan connects that mandate with God.

In his *Studies in the Psychology of Sex*, Havelock Ellis provides an interesting variation on the already much compromised cultural mandate. Ellis declares that

> the sexual act is of no more concern to the community than any other private physiological act . . . but the birth of a child is a social act. Not what goes into the womb but what comes out of it concerns society. The community is invited to receive a new citizen. It is entitled to demand that that citizen . . . shall be properly introduced by a responsible father and a responsible mother. The whole of sexual morality revolves around the child. (417)

Brown argues convincingly for Joyce's fairly extensive knowledge and use of Ellis's *Studies in the Psychology of Sex* (83–88). The passage above from that work typically combines Ellis's apparently liberated views on sexuality with his socialist/eugenicist views on the control of births. While Ellis, who spent his life analyzing and describing sexual acts for the community, ironically argues that the community need not be concerned about sexual acts, he simultaneously insists that the community has a right to demand certain characteristics of the child it accepts.

The setting and circumstances of "Oxen" reflect Ellis's concerns, for the sexual morality of the community in the anteroom of the Holles Street maternity hospital revolves around the birth of the Purefoy baby. Ultimately that community—albeit in parody—celebrates the birth of a new citizen, son of Purefoy, the "conscientious second accountant of the Ulster bank," (*U* 421.2–5: *U* 14.1324). In spite of the forbidden sexual activities linguistically practiced in the episode—most of which have been contraceptive—the ends of the economically and politically dominant Anglo-Irish community have been properly served by the birth of baby Purefoy. Purefoy senior is "the remarkablest progenitor barring none in this chaffering allincluding" episode and all "scholarment" and "Malthusiasts [may] go hang" if they do not agree (*U* 423.24, 29: *U* 14.1411–16).

Ellis begins his discussion of the *science* of procreation as Joyce begins "Oxen," with a rebuttal of the cultural mandate of Genesis, "be fruitful and multiply." Ellis contends that

> humanity has spawned itself ... in thousands of millions of creatures ... a large proportion of whom ... ought never to have been born [and] the voice of Jehovah is now making itself heard through the leaders of mankind in a very different sense.... the question of the procreation of the race [has gained] a new significance [and has even taken on] the character of a new religious movement.... the claim of the race is the claim of religion. (580)

Ellis's voice of Jehovah is echoed and crossbred with the God of Genesis in "Oxen." The religion to which Ellis refers is eugenics, the pseudoscience and theory of social practice that emerged in the late nineteenth and early twentieth centuries. Herbert Spencer, the "guru of Social Darwinism," became its favorite philosopher (Chase 105). Joyce purchased Spencer's *The Study of Sociology* while working on "Oxen" (Ellmann, *Con-*

sciousness 128), and he exposes the pernicious implications of Spencer's and Ellis's theories in "Oxen." Lecky, Shaw, and Webb were all influenced by the doctrines of eugenics, which, reduced to simplest terms, justify classism and racism by pseudoscientific trappings.

Ellis provides a history of Christian attitudes toward sexuality which agrees in the main with Shaw and Lecky (whom Ellis frequently cites). Surprisingly, these accounts are in some sense verified by Noonan, Foucault, and Joyce. Regardless of the point of view or intentions of these writers, each exposes the inherent contradictions in teachings about activities surrounding the sex act. Each writer also exposes, whether consciously or not, an ongoing contest for control over that act. The participants in the contest may from time to time, from age to age, change banners. They usually fall into categories such as church, state, class, or private citizen. Foucault would add "discourse," I believe. Joyce differs from the others, however, in the depth of his coverage, for he brings the reader into the intimate lives of characters struggling with the issues raised in the debate about their right or responsibility to reproduce. The fact that children are more readily "avoidable" (as Shaw puts it) in the twentieth century than ever before seems to have complicated rather than simplified the issues for all of the participants in the debate.

The Blooms are a case in point. For the good of the Empire, the financially secure, healthy, and intelligent Blooms should be producing "hardy annuals" (*U* 161.11: *U* 8.362), as the Purefoys are doing. Except, of course, that the Blooms are Jewish-Irish and not quite as desirable as the Methodist, Anglo-Irish Purefoys. Nor are they really part of the Catholic community of Dublin. Thus, in spite of their economic stability, the Blooms would not be likely to be "naturally selected" by their society to reproduce. On the other hand, Bloom himself would like to have more children, particularly sons, it seems. "I too, last my race. ... No son. Rudy. Too late now. Or if not?" (*U* 285.4–5: *U* 11.1066–67). But apparently Bloom and Molly do not wish to risk another heartbreaking experience like the one they went through with Rudy. "Could never like it [Lombard street or reproductive intercourse?] again after Rudy" (*U* 168.4: *U* 8.610). Because of Rudy's death, it seems, the Blooms practice a form of contraceptive sex which is not clearly intercourse. We know that Bloom indulges in contraceptive sexual activities outside of home. And according to reports submitted to the narrator of "Oxen," Bloom may have become "his own and only enjoyer" (*U* 409.16: *U* 14.914–15). Molly's sexual encounter with Boylan is meant to be a contraceptive one, though she wonders for a moment if she might not have become impregnated. Although she says "I made him pull out," she wonders if after the last time when she "let him finish it in" her, she has washed out all the sperm. Her attitude about the possibility of being pregnant is equivocal; the idea is at first apparently distasteful, but later she thinks "supposing I risked having another ... Poldy has more spunk in him yes thatd be awfully jolly" (*U* 742.33–34: *U* 18.155–68).

The Blooms, then, incorporate the propagatory conflicts inherent in a neo-Malthusian postwar society. Their own personal laws might have them be fruitful and multiply, but at the same time they employ various contraceptive practices or devices to avoid the risk of having another child who might not survive. Bloom's "rubber preservative," always at the ready, is as much a barrier to his freedom of expression as it is a symbol of sexual liberation. Joyce underscores that irony in "Oxen," where one of the alternative names for Preservative is Killchild.

The crime in "Oxen" is committed by and perpetrated on civilization. Joyce called the crime fraud, a common name for contraception. But fraud also means deceit, insincerity, and false representation. The players in "Oxen" are each in a way guilty of fraud because the culture has made it impossible for them to honestly carry out its inscrutable mandate. The narrator, perhaps representing that mandate, attempts to make us see the characters as he wishes us to see them, tries to make us condemn or praise according to his lights. The medical profession is guilty because, while empowered to preserve life, it provides the information and means necessary to cheat fecundity. The Church is guilty by valuing celibacy and paradoxically encouraging fertility. Language itself is guilty because it obscures the truth.

"Oxen" might be compared to the Bradlaugh–Besant trial, where the issue of contraception was put into discourse. Nowhere until the *Wake* are societal attitudes about population control more comprehensively treated and "tried" by Joyce than in "Oxen." But "Oxen" is more realistic than that real-life trial, for "Oxen" shows that regardless of one's stance, individual choices are pressured in such a way that they become less than free. The ironic tone of "Oxen" (typical of postwar narrative voices) toward the sexually liberated participants in the episode matches Foucault's tone at the conclusion of *The History of Sexuality:* "The irony of [the deployment of sexuality] is in having us believe that our 'liberation' is in the balance" (159).

Most of the components of "Oxen" had been available to Joyce for years. He had acquired nearly all the works I have cited in this chapter long before "Oxen" was produced. The birth control movement had been underway for forty years. Malthusianism had passed the century mark, and Genesis is ageless. The inspiration for combining these elements, however, may have come from a unique concurrence of events, the most significant of which was the conclusion of a war that made the controversy about sterilizing individual acts of coition an absurd "strife of tongues" (*U* 410.19: *U* 14.952).

4

Birth Control on Trial

"Unless sexual science is incorporated as an integral part of world statesmanship and the importance of Birth Control is recognized, [efforts to create a] new civilization are foredoomed to failure"
—Margaret Sanger, *The Pivot of Civilization* 140.

In any scientific assessment of a population's stability, the most significant variables are birth, death, and migration rates (both emigration and immigration). But even scientific assessments, though presumed to be objective, are inevitably altered by the weight of tacit ideological assumptions. Among such assumptions, pressures for socially coherent demographic behavior were especially numerous, strong, and contradictory during the 1920s and 1930s. Each of these variables was invoked by one faction or another to make a case for population control. Post–World War I polemics, the birth control movement (1876–1931), sexologists, eugenicists, and psychoanalysts all contributed to the babel about procreative activity.

Unprecedented war losses and the consequent decline in reproduction rates inspired particularly strong populationist programs in Germany, Italy, Belgium, and France. Between the wars, "France's population growth was (with the exception of Ireland) the lowest in Europe" (Dyer 64). Thus, pro-birth agitation was strongest in the country where James Joyce happened to be living and producing *Finnegans Wake*. Concurrently, the birth control movement—libertarian and feminist in nature—traveled from England to America and back to the Continent, gaining force as it grew. The often contradictory rhetoric of these movements epitomizes the conflict at the very heart of population control, indeed at the heart of all conflict—the individual versus the collective will. The right to liberty and self-determination, specifically in procreative and migratory activities, became especially ambiguous during the transitional demographic conditions brought about by the First World War as it had become in Joyce's Ireland since the Famine. The interwar populationist rhetoric in France typifies the pressure brought to bear on the individual citizen and compares with the rhetorical ploys used in turn-of-the-century Ireland. For example, in 1928, a member of the French Chamber of Deputies warned that "a new peril, as formidable as the German army, looms before us ... the demographic peril, the slow but continuous and mortal bleeding of this country" (Dyer 78). The anemia metaphor recalls the emigration tropes used in Irish journals, histories, and sermons during Joyce's youth.

In 1929 the magazine *L'Illustration* undertook a two-year study of the population problem in France. In January of that year, the magazine had expressed a commonly held fear that "if population continues at the present rate, in half a century, it is calculated, there will no longer be a single inhabitant of French origin" (Dyer 78). Thus does the instinct of the state, ethnic group, social class, or religious sect to "protect" itself from extinction subtly and inexorably challenge the individual's right to determine the number of progeny she will produce. On the other hand, during these same interwar decades, procreative activity, an engendering process in every sense of the word in Western culture—establishing masculine and (more explicitly) feminine identity as well as familial roles—was under continued scrutiny and revaluation. In spite of the populationist propaganda in France, "contraception had become an epidemic" (Dyer 81), and sexual activity was being touted by birth control advocates and sexologists as "a psychic and spiritual avenue of expression" not necessarily intended for reproduction (Sanger, *Pivot* 140).

The ensuing debate raised issues about the rights and duties of the ideal state, family, and citizen—male and female—which remain unresolved even today. While attitudes about the makeup of a "typical" family in Western society varied in postwar Europe, there was widespread concern that the family unit not be allowed to break down lest the nation follow. In France, the *Code de la Famille*, which was established as law in 1939, resulted from such concerns and specifically provided financial support for couples who increased the size of their families. Even before its formalization, such a policy had been advocated in the press for years as a means of rebuilding the population after the war. Ironically, the law was codified in July, between the occupation of Prague and the invasion of Poland, and coincidentally just two months after the publication of *Finnegans Wake*. Pre-codification arguments in the press about the implications of passing such a law were certainly available for

Joyce to draw on while writing the *Wake*. While those arguments featured an emphasis on the mother's role as the regenerator of French civilization, other works, such as Alexander Morris Carr-Saunders, *The Population Problem: A Study in Human Evolution,* and David Victor Glass, *Population Policies and Movements in Europe,* indicate the continuing universal interest in questions of population control, the inevitable ideological "stamps" of various population policies, and the tendency to look to the family as the place where the problem would be solved. Margaret Sanger's 1942 decision to change the name of the Birth Control Federation to the Planned Parenthood Federation, for instance, indicates societal concern about the threat to family stability apparently posed by the birth control movement.

Inevitably, because it is an Irish family history produced in France, the *Wake* absorbs and refracts the complex issues in the population debate. In fact, the *Wake* is *about* the three variables of demographics—birth, death, and migration—and the consequences of society's manipulation of attitudes toward those variables. It represents the tragicomic situation of father, mother, brother(s), and sister(s) attempting to respond to the demands of an amorphous culture that sends extraordinarily mixed and constantly changing messages about not only the value of life, but also the formation of identities of all kinds, national, familial, and sexual. The members of the *Wake*'s "typical" Western family, then, are attempting to conduct their lives according to some shifting design discernible yet inscrutable to both themselves and their community.

Not surprisingly, the various themes involved in population control that are introduced in the first book of the *Wake* are elaborated throughout. John Gordon points out that one of the *Wake*'s dreamers is the "exiled" (read also emigrant) James Joyce, whose "elopement" from Ireland to Europe remained the decisive event of his and Nora's lives (96). Emigration from and return to Ireland is established as a major framework of the book in the emblematic opening paragraphs, where Sir Tristam has "rearrived from North Amorica" (*FW* 3.5). In Joyce's working out of this returning exile theme, Gordon reads sympathy for Nora's emigrant sensibilities (enthusiasm about leaving/longing to return) as well as for Joyce's own divided feelings about deserting father and homeland. "To part from Devlin," the *Wake* declares, "is hard as Nugent knew" (*FW* 24.25–26).

The letter in book 1, chapter 5 that according to Patrick McCarthy represents the *Wake* ("Structures" 597) becomes entangled in the emigration theme by virtue of its suspected source, an Irish emigrant now living in Boston. Shaun will be bound for America and Shem for Europe before the *Wake* circles back on itself. And, in book 1, chapter 3, "Earwicker, that patternmind, that paradigmatic ear ... behind faminebuilt walls ... mourn[s] the flight of his wild guineese" (*FW* 70.75–71.5). Earwicker's wild guineese hark back to the wild geese, Irish refugees of the Famine, publicly mourned in 1907 by Joyce in "Ireland, Island of Saints and Sages" (*CW* 172).

Earwicker's regretful musings implicate him not only in the emigration theme, but also in the legacy of the Famine which had helped to build the walls that divide this Anglo-Irish tavern keeper from his customers. Earwicker's superior, ascendant social position alienates him from the frequenters of his tavern as the Famine had alienated Protestant landlord from Catholic tenant, and those who fled Ireland from those who remained. HCE's estrangement from the "people" had already been suggested at 45.14 where, as Persse O'Reilly, he is accused of promoting "immaculate contraceptives for the populace." "Populace," incorporating the Pope and the populous, suggests the official anti-contraceptive attitude of the Catholic majority. Birth control, as a basic type of population control, emerges as an important motif in the *Wake*.

The feminine principle in the form of the family hen enters early in the *Wake* via the patterings and musings of the same Earwicker (that patternmind) cited above. As she becomes anthropomorphized as a wife and mother, a number of conventions about the role of women in the alleged population crisis of the 1920s and 1930s are revealed. Significantly, as conjured by Earwicker, the engendering conventions are masculine. We find that she is afraid of "Thon's flash [and] toomcracks [and] all the deed in the woe" (*FW* 11.4–7). From her fear of violence and concern about the war dead, she is furthermore classified as a "peacefugle" (*FW* 11.9). She makes her appearance as "the armitides toonigh" and thus the likelihood of a "muddy kissmans to the minutia workers" is great (*FW* 11.13–15). The "gorgeups truce" expected to follow the impending armistice and fighting men's return from the trench mud to the waiting lips of female munitions workers promises "happinest childher everwere."

The ironic role assigned women during and following the "war to end all wars" informs the whole passage. The peace-loving nature of the woman is undercut by her role as munitions worker, thus she is a "peacefugle" (the OED defines a "fugle" as both a cheat and a model soldier) or a good soldier who cheats peace. Just as she is called upon to produce the arms to kill men during the war, she is expected following the war to willingly and happily reproduce children everywhere. Bonnie Kime Scott's observation about the community of women in the "Nausicaa" episode of *Ulysses* is relevant here to the role of wife and mother presented in this opening section of the *Wake:* "Even working in their own territory, and with the ethics of nurture and peace ... women preserve the gender roles of males in society and discourse" (*James Joyce* 65).

Edmund Epstein suggests that contemporary events such as the Armistice may give some clue as to what inspired Joyce to write the *Wake*. We know that he was thinking about it in the autumn of 1922, and "it may have been Armistice Day, November 11, 1922, that started him thinking about conflict" (Epstein 26). Surely, it is just before that Armistice when Earwicker musingly anticipates and unwittingly assigns to woman (just as much of the postwar propaganda was doing) the task of revitalizing the civilization she had so recently been called upon to help destroy. We learn at 11.33 that "her birth is uncontrollable"; but we are also told at 12.11 that she is a "turfwoman," making her closely related to the composite female birth control advocate who will be tried in book 3, chapter 4. This woman Earwicker has conjured therefore incorporates features of the historical "tough" woman increasingly more willing to stand up for the right to control her births.

The most notorious, most effective, and toughest of these birth control advocates in the twentieth century was Margaret Sanger. Her assertion, made in 1922, that the entire world was "being permeated with the message of birth control" (*New Motherhood* 354) was well-founded, due in great measure to her own efforts. In 1927 at the World Population Conference in Geneva, Sanger brought together "leading demographers, scientists, sociologists and physicians" from around the world (Fryer 219). She published and lectured profusely, stood trial repeatedly, and claimed to have coined the term "birth control" in 1911 (Gray 72). She appears in Jaun's sermon as "Population Peg" (*FW* 436.10), along with her two British counterparts, Marie Stopes (*FW* 444.8) and Annie Besant, "Annybettyelsas" (*FW* 444.31).

The latter two British zealots had also firmly established reputations in the birth control movement. Stopes's *Married Love,* published first in America and then in London in 1918, was an immediate bestseller. But Stopes received more inquiries about the brief section on contraception than about the major subject of the book, how to achieve satisfying sex in marriage. (Maude 135–67). Like Sanger, Stopes responded to the obvious need of women to regulate their reproductive lives by publishing, lecturing, and opening clinics where contraceptives were distributed. And, like Sanger, she was repeatedly brought to trial for her trouble. Of the three women who pioneered the birth control movement, however, Annie Besant's influence was felt earliest. Her joint trial with Charles Bradlaugh in 1874 for publishing *The Fruits of Philosophy* brought birth control to public attention and led to the founding of the Malthusian League. The *Wake*, then, is permeated with the message of birth control, as the world was, largely because of the influence of these three pioneer "birth controllers" (as I shall call them after Peter Fryer's work of that title).

The direction taken by much of the work of Sanger and Stopes was determined by the intense opposition to birth control expressed in various quarters in the 1920s and 1930s, when the most formidable opponents of the movement were the European populationists and the Roman Catholic Church. The Church's response, summarized in the encyclical *Casti Connubii*, was published in December 1930 in reaction to the cautious approval afforded birth control by the Protestant Episcopal Church at the Lambeth Conference (Noonan, *Contraception* 409). Meanwhile, in Ireland, the Censorship of Publications Act of 1929 made it a crime to print, publish, sell, or distribute "any book or periodical which advocates or might be supposed to advocate the unnatural prevention of conception" (Noonan, *Contraception* 411). Naturally the *Wake* reflects the opposition as well as the defense and, moreover, reconstructs the contradictions and coincidences in the historical arguments about birth control. Furthermore, the *Wake* demonstrates, as did the birth controllers and their opponents, that birth control is part of the larger issue of population control, which in turn is concerned with the survival of the species. With the birth control movement as backdrop, in the remainder of this chapter I hope to show how and why the *Wake* is riddled with pro and con contraceptive and populationist rhetoric, allusions, and "performances."

Within the *Wake*, during a "period of pure lyricism of shame-bred music," Professor Jones "advises any unborn singer who may still be among my heeders to forget her temporal diaphragm at home" (*FW* 164.35–36). Because both Sanger and Stopes frequently and publicly encouraged the use of diaphragms (rather than condoms or *coitus interruptus*) for birth control purposes, I am tempted to read "singer" as "Sanger" here and to interpret this passage, and indeed the whole section from 164.6–167.3 (Professor Jones's lecture), as a commentary on the birth control agitation these two women came to represent. A later reference in the *Wake* that conflates the hen and HCE substantiates my reading: "And insodaintily she's a quine of selm ashaker while as a murder of corpse when his *magot's* up he's the best berrathon *sanger* in all the aisles of Skaldignavia" (*FW* 254.31–33; emphasis mine). Under the ae-

gis of the Blessed Virgin (represented by the Sodality), this passage sub-
sumes birth control (represented by Sanger), zero population growth
(represented by the Shakers), and the attitude that birth control represents a type of murder. Significantly, "berrathon sanger" readily trans-
lates into "baritone singer," reversing the situation in the Professor Jones
passage quoted above.

Professor Jones proposes that the "too males pooles," that is, the
two opposite male brothers about whom he has been speaking, "must
waistfully woent a female to focus." The wistful desire of this divided
male psyche reflects the blurring of the female role (the female is both
difficult to focus on and difficult to procreate with) between the wars.
That female turns out to be "the cowrymaid M." or "Margareen" (*FW*
164.6–14). The similarity between "Margareen" and "Margaret" makes
even stronger the likelihood that "Sanger" is a prototype of "singer."
"Margareen" may also incorporate "Marie" Stopes, who regretted that
women had been taught to feel ashamed ("shame-bred") of their periods
of heightened sexual desire. "In civilized countries," Stopes wrote,
"knowledge of the needs of both sexes have [sic] been lost—and nothing
but a muffled confusion of individual gossip disturbs a silence, shame-
faced or foul" (*Married Love* 14). Stopes wrote of women's periods of
heightened desire in terms which might very well be described as "pure
lyricism." Her medical studies and observation of "patients" led her to
create a graph showing the "Law of Periodicity of Recurrence of Desire
in Women" (*Married Love* 174). At the very least, "Margareen" suggests a
young Irish woman who has learned the value of a diaphragm through
the efforts of women like Sanger and Stopes.

The Professor first suggests fellatio as an alternative to the use of
the diaphragm, "attack the roulade with a swift *colpo di glottide* to the lug
[and] O! to cluse her eyes and aiopen her oath and see what spice I may
send her" (*FW* 165.1–5), and then goes on to describe other, more effi-
cient types of contraceptives. The recurrent allusions to various, apparently fantastic, forms of contraceptives in the *Wake* reflects historical
reality. "By 1935 some two hundred types of mechanical devices, either
condoms or pessaries, were in use in Western societies, and a wide range
of chemicals was being employed as spermicides or occlusive agents;
contraception was now a substantial business" (Noonan, "Contraception" 211).

In the course of his lecture, the Professor invokes the name of Annie Besant, who appears as "a lunger planner's byscent" (165.10) and
"lady Trabezond (Marge in her *excelsis*)" (165.22). Thus, "byscent" and
"bezond" are alternative versions of her sis, "Marge," whom she possibly

excels and certainly preceded. "Lady Trabezond" seems to have taken part in the invention of contraceptive "hatboxes" and the "climactogram." The latter may owe something to Stopes's periodicity chart. In any case, the Professor claims to be inventing "a more patent process, foolproof and pryperfect" (FW 165.31–32).

Having invented a better product, the Professor metaphorically sizes up the customer who will use it: "that demilitery young female (we will continue to call her Marge) whose types may be met with in any public garden" (FW 166.4–6). The female is here endowed with characteristics of the militant feminist or the female after the war, or both. As the passage continues, she becomes a type of Gerty MacDowell conventionalized by ladies' journalese. However, the references to "muffin cap" and "angelskin," and the fact that she is "ovidently on the look out for 'him' " (FW 166.8–12) reveal that the Professor is still discussing contraceptives. The passage, narrated in a masculine voice, also reveals two types of cultural ambivalence: the reluctance of a patriarchal society to allow young women the freedom and control that female contraceptives allow; and the reluctance on the part of young women themselves to give up entirely the dependent and frivolous image they have been assigned.

Those ambivalent attitudes, with emphasis on the patriarchal position, are specifically expressed in the next paragraph: "for the femininny of that totamulier will always lack the musculink of a verumvirum. My solotions for the proper parturience of matres and the education of micturious mites must stand over from the moment till I tackle this tickler hussy for occupying my uttentions" (FW 166.29ff.). From the outset of their campaign, the femininity and maternal instincts of the birth controllers were questioned, and their contention that young girls ("micturious mites") should be taught birth control methods even before marriage was vigorously attacked. This passage, then, seems to echo those attacks while also making the point that many of the arguments against birth control were in fact ad hominem arguments against the individual birth controller ("this tickler hussy") herself.

Finally, the Professor sums up this cowrymaid, Margareen, as "a cleopatrician in her own right [who] at once complicates the position while Burrus and Caseous are contending for her misstery" (FW 166.34–36). Burrus and Caseous may here represent not only patriarchal factions within the "state" of Western culture—contending for the right to control feminine procreative power—but also the confusion felt by the well-intentioned male who simply wants to understand how to treat modern woman. In the latter case, the composite Burrus and Caseous is an extension of Leopold Bloom, who spent a great deal of Bloomsday wondering how to treat his Cleopatra.

We next meet the three birth controllers in Jaun's sermon (*FW* 432.4–446.26), where his references to them once again signal a treatment of patriarchal attitudes toward women's increasing awareness of their own power over population growth. Though the sermon is more comprehensive than Professor Jones's lecture, covering a wider range of population issues, Jaun's position is more blatantly chauvanistic and ultimately ethnocentric. This is not surprising since Jaun is a lecherous Irish/French priest here preaching to the twenty-nine schoolgirls from "Benet Saint Berched's *national* nightschool" (*FW* 430.2; emphasis mine).

Besant's name crops up early in the sermon when Jaun is trying to decide on the first subject he will cover, "rubrics, mandarimus, pasqualines, or veridads . . . and, for the lover of lithurgy, bekant or besant" (*FW* 432.31–33). Besant may legitimately appear along with Pascal, Bacon, Kant, and "true fathers" because of her fame as a Theosophist, a pseudo-theologian-philosopher, but evidence in the rest of the sermon suggests that Joyce also intended to invoke her earlier work for birth control. Joyce's placement of her in the company of such men argues for the importance of the movement she helped to start—in his mind as influential as the ideas of Pascal, Kant, and even the laws (rubrics) of the Church—but also may be meant to highlight the fact that Besant later deserted that cause for Theosophy.

Following a lengthy travesty of the ten commandments and all manner of lesser mandates of the Church, Jaun gives his version of the Church's teaching about legitimate sexual activity. Jaun's interpretation includes references to incest and prostitution, "cisternbrothelly," and to "love through the usual channels" or "canalised love." The terms "usual channels" and "canalised" echo Joyce's references in *Exiles* (*E* 173) and *Ulysses* (*U* 223.31: *U* 10.168) to the Church's definition of the proper receptacle for the sperm of a married man: *emissio seminis inter vas naturale.* It is not clear whether Jaun is preaching for or against the limitation of sexual activity to usual channels; he does seem, however, to insist on establishing some kind of parameters that keep him in control of the girls' (and especially his sister's) sex life. Otherwise, he says, "I'll be apt to flail that tail for you till it's borning" (*FW* 436.36–437.1).

This part of the sermon is introduced by an ambiguous reference to "Population Peg" (Sanger) and a clearer reference to the notion that women become promiscuous during wartime. "While there's men-a'war on the say there'll be loves-o'women on the do" (*FW* 436.10–15). Perhaps the inference to be made is that contraceptives encourage such promiscuity. At any rate, Jaun eventually turns to the subject of "the marriage slump that's on in this oil age and pulexes three shillings a pint and wives at six and seven when domestic calamities belame par and newlaids bellow mar for the twenty twotoosent time" (*FW* 438.21–24). Here, the rhetoric parodies press coverage in France of the interwar population crisis.

Birthrates in France during those years were the lowest in the world, 400,000 abortions were performed annually (even though the government had prohibited abortion and the sale of contraceptives), the number of marriages diminished sharply, women far outnumbered men, and the rise in divorces was maintained (Dyer 79–80). One paradoxical reason for the low birthrate, given to journalist Ludovic Nadeau in 1929, was that the French were "too rich and too poor" to have children. Couples who did marry postponed having children until they felt wealthy enough to support them (Dyer 81). Jaun's later remark about the "fear and love of gold" (*FW* 438.31) seems to capitalize on that paradox. Gold here becomes both wealth and sperm.

In spite of his obvious awareness of the population crisis, Jaun warns his sister not to have sexual intercourse, "If ever I catch you at it, mind, it's you that will cocottch it!" (*FW* 439.3–4). The guilty stutter inherited from his father is evident here, and as the sermon continues, it becomes more and more clear that Jaun wants to have Issy to himself. He does promise her that once she is married much of the sexual activity that has been forbidden her by the Church will be allowed. "When the gong goes for hornets-two-nest marriage step into your harness and strip that nullity suit. Faminy, hold back! For the race is to the rashest of, the romping, jomping rushes of" (*FW* 441.1–4). Both the ecclesiastical and the populationist attitudes are revealed in this passage. Once married, the couple, in harness, should attempt to win the race. The race to be won, or saved, of course, is the particular population in distress. Sanctions against premarital sexual activity as well as contraceptive devices ("nullity" suits) must be stripped off. Famine can be held back or risked by the family that rashly reproduces. Jaun repeats the theme several lines later, this time with even more obvious reference to populationist and official Catholic attitudes in Ireland and France: "You can down all the dripping you can dumple to ... ad libidinum, in these lassitudes if you've parents and things to look after. That was what stuck to the Comtesse Cantilene while she was sticking out Mavis Toffeelips to feed her soprannated huspals, and it is henceforth associated with her names" (*FW* 441.8–11). The irony of the Church's position (a bit oversimplified here) is that married couples who may already be overburdened with responsibility (being parents with things to look after) can indulge their libidos ad infinitum while unmarried young people who have no responsibilities cannot. The "Comtesse Cantilene" is a Frenchified version of Yeats's Countess Cathleen who sold her soul to the devil in order to save the peasants from famine. There seems to be an implicit attack here on a Church or State that will encourage a population to grow beyond its means to survive and condemn the means of checking or preserving that same population.

Jaun moves abruptly from the subject of marital sex to a tirade on divorce. The subject seems to become confused with the issue of cross-cultural marriage, and Jaun's desire for his sister comes to typify a sort of xenophobia (*FW* 441.24–444.5). He eventually gets back to the subject of extramarital sex and the use of contraceptives, however, reintroducing the topics with a reference to Marie Stopes: "It may all be topping fun but it's tip and run and touch and flow for every whack when Marie stopes Phil fluther's game to go" (*FW* 444.7–8). The reference to Stopes may be based on her advice that each married pair "must, using the tenderest and most delicate touches, sound and test each other," each touch causing a "fluid" response (*Married Love* 174).

Stopes believed that the "harmonious intermingling" of male and female fluids during intercourse was highly desirable and healthful. In *A New Gospel to All Peoples*, Stopes wrote that "in order not to thwart the other designs and purposes of the sex act ... the means used to control conception must permit of the entry, the mingling and the mutual exchange of secretions between the man's uncovered organ and the woman's" (quoted in Fryer 228). Jaun's "mingling of our meeting waters" (446.14) mentioned later in the sermon is a version of the doctrine Stopes popularized.

Jaun continues to give advice about "misconception" (unplanned pregnancy) and "plightforlifer" (a marriage brought about by an unplanned pregnancy). To avoid such eventualities, Jaun advises the use of a birth control device: "You better keep in the barrel straight around vokseburst as I recommence to you" (*FW* 444.11–17). Later in the same passage Jaun refers to "Annybettyelsas," (Annie Besant) and accuses his sister of having taken part in contraceptive sex on "dates with slickers"; he threatens to "tear up [her] limpshades and lock all [her] trotters in the closet [and] cut [her] silkskin into garters" (*FW* 444.33–445.4–5).

Finally, it becomes clear that behind all these warnings about Issy's sexual behavior and all this advice about contraceptives is Jaun's intention to keep Issy pure so that he may some day return and breed with her. "Aerwenger's my breed so may we uncreepingly multipede like the sands on Amberhann!" (*FW* 445.36–446.1). Earlier, Jaun had espoused certain eugenicist and even racist doctrines (*FW* 443), asserting that "We are all eyes," that he might even carry out a "progromme," "and pitch in and swing for your perfect stranger." The Aerwenger passage seems to be an extension of these notions. The perfect stranger becomes Jaun himself (he is all "eye" or "I") and will multiply with his own kind (the "Aerwinger" or Earwicker family), even, it would seem, to the extinction of other breeds or races. Thus, birth control is carried to its apparently absurd extreme. The idea becomes more frightening than absurd, however, when considered in the light of Hitler's interpretation of eugenicist doctrines and his influence on German attitudes toward racial purity.

Jaun's sermon exemplifies Sanger's contention that "even the minister, seeking to keep abreast of the times, proclaims [birth control] from the pulpit" (*New Motherhood* 354). Sanger also believed that the Church (like Jaun) subverted its own message by insuring that birth control would continue to be discussed publicly. Interestingly, Richard Brown aligns Jaun's sermon with the bull-session section of "Oxen." Brown suggests that like the titillating confessors in "Oxen," Jaun overtly advises orthodox reproductive sex, yet "somehow, forbidden contraceptive information leaks out" (73).

Jaun's sermon also epitomizes the irony of the birth control movement in another way. While the birth controllers advocated responsible *parenting*, the contraceptive devices they advertised made respectable and "safe" the sort of promiscuous sexual relations that Jaun, the "celibate" priest, describes to his young virgin sister. In spite of its expressed intention to promote solid marital relations and conscious begetting, then, the birth control movement, like Jaun's homily, made a considerable contribution to the deployment of sexuality for the sake of sexual power and pleasure.

If the doctrines and practices that the pioneer birth controllers advocated are propagated and parodied, puffed up and punctured in Jaun's sermon and elsewhere in the *Wake*, equally so are the responses of the loudest and most consistent of their critics, the Catholic Church. As late as 1959, Aldous Huxley expected to be taken seriously when he asserted that "the Catholic Church is the one so far insuperable obstacle to the solution of the world's population problems. On a reversal of its attitude may hang the survival of our society" (Introduction, Sulloway *xix*). Huxley echoed a host of writers, including Sanger and Stopes, who saw the Church as a major cause of surplus population, poverty, and the continued enslavement of women. It is, of course, as Catholic priest and finally as papal nuncio that Jaun delivers his sermon on population control.

In addition to the numerous contraceptive allusions in Professor Jones's lecture and in Jaun's sermon, a concentrated rash of similar references breaks out in book 3, chapter 4, the close-up of the Porter family. As Joyce does throughout the *Wake*, he overloads the language here with topical allusions that establish the dominant characteristics of the time and space he is attempting to reproduce. In the Porter chapter, that time is close to the consciousness of the dreamer, and close to the present (the 1920s and 1930s). The bedrooms of the Porter family take up the space of the episode. Given that time and space, the activity of the married pair is predictably contraceptive. Appropriately, among the furnishings of the bedroom is a "man's gummy article, pink" (*FW* 559.15–16). The gummy article and the cultural convention it typifies will henceforth play a major role in the episode.

Early in the chapter, we learn that the Porters are "in their bed of trial, on the bolster of hardship ... under coverlets of cowardice ... his mace of might mortified, her beautifell hung up on a nail (*FW* 558.26–29). The bed of trial might be interpreted as the sexual life of the Western world, a rotting foundation ("bed") of contraceptive sexual activity, where the contraceptive devices become "coverlets of cowardice." The husband's "mace of might" (penis) is "mortified," that is, stiff with sexual desire, but humiliatingly unproductive, truly an instrument of death. The wife's "beautifell" (artificial hair) is "hung up on a nail," (a cold, rigid device). The emphasis of the whole passage (especially the reference to "the bolster of hardship") recalls the condemnation of non-reproductive sexuality in *Casti Connubii*, where first consideration in marriage is assigned to "the offspring, which many have the boldness to call the disagreeable burden of matrimony" (quoted in Fremantle 239).

In their contraceptive bed of trial, bolstered (justified) by hardship, the modern Porters recall certain "component partners of our societate" (*FW* 142.8) described in book 1, chapter 6, the riddle chapter: "Latecomers ... the porters of the passions ... who crunch the crusts of comfort due to depredation ... condone every evil by practical justification and condam any good to its own gratification" (*FW* 142.16–23). Joyce is playing with "condom" here, I believe, transforming the contraceptive device into a symbol of permissiveness and self-gratification justified by practical considerations. Again, the sound and sense of the passage echoes *Casti Conubii* and the long line of ecclesiastical anti-contraceptive pronouncements upon which that encyclical is based.

Margaret Solomon makes three observations about the Porter chapter: it is "about watching"; it is "a period of sterility"; and yet, it "is as filled with anticipation as it is with degeneration" (201–2). Each of

Solomon's points is relevant to the birth control movement which helped produce the chapter. In effect, the birth controllers invited the public—especially women who had not had easy access to "sex" books in the past—to take a closer look at ("watch") every aspect of the sexual act. Respectable people could now legitimately investigate the sexual activities of others in order to gain important information about how to control the growth of their own families in particular and population in general. The "simple statements [of *Married Love* were] based on a very large number of observations. . . . For many years many men and women have confided in me the secrets of their lives" (*Married Love* 12, 28–29), Stopes wrote, as she proceeded to reveal those secrets to a curious public.

The birth controllers quite naturally turned to the most blatant of all voyeurs, the sexologists, for information and guidance. A case in point is the mutual admiration and professional support reciprocated by Marie Stopes and Margaret Sanger on one hand, and Havelock Ellis on the other. Ellis's seven-volume *Studies in the Psychology of Sex,* though detailed and fascinating, was not widely read by middle-class couples. In contrast, the inexpensive, brief, but numerous works of Stopes and Sanger—which were based in part on Ellis's findings—went into multiple reprintings. Ellis wrote introductions for the works of both women and thus participated in their success, while they were able to justify the voyeuristic implications of their work by citing his authority. Margot Norris observes that in the *Wake,* "the copulation of III.4 is witnessed through the eye of the professional observer: the social worker . . . the lawyer . . . the tour guide" (87). I would add the sexologist and the birth control advocate. Undoubtedly, Joyce stations "Watchman Havelook" near the opening of the Porter chapter in recognition of the voyeuristic link between contraception and sexology.

Margaret Solomon's designation of the Porter chapter as a "period of sterility" is one with which most critics seem to agree, at least to the extent that the chapter depicts a contraceptive sexual act. Yet like all of the *Wake,* and in spite of its sterile atmosphere, the chapter exhibits an inordinate interest in sexual activity. In fact, the chapter raises the question originally posed in *Ulysses* of whether "sterile" sex can be completely satisfying. Near the end of the chapter, thanks are proffered to "his auricular of Malthus, the promethean paratonnerwetter which first (Pray go! pray go!) taught love's lightning the way, (pity shown) to, well, conduct itself (mercy, good shot! only please don't mention it!)" (*FW* 585.11–14). The admiration for Malthus, credited here with having started the whole campaign for contraceptive sex (in fact he did not), however, is equivocal. Likewise, Annuska's reproach to Humperfeldt,

"You never wet the tea!" (*FW* 585.31), indicates dissatisfaction with sterile copulation, or at the very least, copulation with a condom rather than a diaphragm.

The birth controllers pointed out that sexual intercourse without the fear of pregnancy is often more satisfying, especially to the woman, than otherwise. Furthermore, the diaphragm allows for the "wetting of the tea" so important to both parties, and the man need never know the diaphragm is in place. The Porter chapter does not bear out these arguments of the birth controllers, however. Here, contraceptive sex by any other name is sterile sex and can never completely satisfy the reproductive urge that motivates every coupling. Accordingly, near the end of the chapter, the wife's fear that the husband will break the condom is no fear at all, but a wish that, by means of a "slip," her unborn babies will "waken": "Goeasyosey, for the grace of the fields, or hooley pooley, cuppy, we'll both be bye and by caught in the slips for fear he'd tyre and burst his dunlops and waken her bornybarnies making his boobybabies" (*FW* 584.11−16).

The degeneration of the Porters, as Solomon points out, is anticipatory. Their implicit dissatisfaction with contraception heightens that sense of anticipation and conveys an attitude toward the recycling of civilization which may have become clear to Joyce while he was writing "Oxen." Joyce never lost sight of that "command and promise which on all mortals with prophecy of abundance or with diminution's menace that exalted of reiteratedly procreating function ever irrevocably enjoined" (*U* 383.34−37: *U* 14.29−32). Even though the *Wake* reproduces all sides of the debate about birth control, its final position is that the urge to give birth will generally prevail over the desire for "pure" sex. A central passage of *Casti Connubii* asserts that "to circumscribe in any way the principal ends of marriage laid down in the beginning by God Himself in the words 'Increase and multiply,' is beyond the power of any human law" (quoted in Fremantle 236). Putting aside the convention of marriage, the *Wake* seems to concur with this point of view: the urge to reproduce the species is beyond the control of human law, maybe even of human understanding. On the other hand, the *Wake* shows that individual men and women have always attempted to control birth. So have they attempted to separate the pleasure of sex from its productivity.

The societies to which those individuals belong, however, have challenged their right to exercise that control. Thus the "crime" of contraception has a long history, throughout which birth control has been tried in every variety of court. Contraception was on trial in the press in the 1920s and 1930s. It was also on trial in sermons, pamphlets, Marxist propaganda, medical journals, and political speeches. Nearly every type of organization found that it had a stake in the outcome of the case.

Accordingly, then, during "the second position of discordance" (Mark's version of history) in the Porter chapter, there occurs "the commonest of all cases arising out of umbrella history in connection with the wood industries in our courts of litigation" (*FW* 573.35–574.1). I will interpret this section (in the future to be called the "Umbrella Case") against the background of the cases which Annie Besant, Margaret Sanger, and Marie Stopes fought both in and out of court, demonstrating that even as it builds on historical coincidence and repetition, the *Wake* reflects its real time quite accurately.

"Umbrella history," as it is called in the *Wake*, might be interpreted to mean universal history, but in light of Joyce's use of umbrellas, raincoats, galoshes, and other waterproofing devices as symbolic contraceptives, he clearly means to put birth control on trial. Furthermore, because "umbrella" suggests an all-encompassing category, I would argue that population control is being tried. Some of the composite participants in the Umbrella Case are easy to identify; others are more difficult, for the world and times Joyce lived in abounded in models for judge, jury, defendants, and prosecutor. Yet the characters I have identified in the conflict are as accurate as such as amorphous case will allow. In fact, the participants in real-life birth control cases often changed places. Sanger, for example, was usually on trial for breaking an obscenity law, but she took the police department and the Catholic Church in New York City to court in 1921 for obstructing her right to free speech (Gray 173–75). Similarly, Marie Stopes sued and was sued for libel in cases involving her belief that a Roman Catholic conspiracy to control the press (by way of Ireland) was afoot (Maude 206–27).

Joyce frequently uses trials in the *Wake* and elsewhere ("Circe," for example) to question conventional wisdom and prejudices. Ironically, the trial (like confession) encourages the exposure of otherwise censored topics, thereby undercutting the law it seeks to support. Bernard Benstock observes that "the important trial that attempts to get to the bottom of the epic event of Earwicker's fall is constantly being replayed, each time amassing new evidence on top of evidence already obscured. ... each age interprets the significance of the epic fall in its own terms to satisfy its own needs and desires" (*Joyce-Again's Wake* 194). The Umbrella Case, like the other trials in the *Wake*, builds on the past, but highlights the terms of its present.

The trials of the birth controllers were both present and accessible to Joyce; many made front-page news for weeks at a time. Several, like those of Sanger and Stopes, were recounted in best-selling biographical works in the 1930s. Like the sections and chapters of the *Wake* itself, the records of these trials are amazingly, even laughably, repetitious and confusing. In analyzing the Umbrella Case, I will juxtapose the characters, events, or attitudes suggested in the *Wake* with real events and attitudes reported about the trials of the birth controllers and the response of the Catholic Church.

The narrator of the Umbrella Case introduces it as "perhaps the commonest of all cases arising out of umbrella history in connection with the wood industries in our courts of litigation" (*FW* 573.35–574.1). The "wood industries" are clearly related to all other forest and tree references in the *Wake*, and the phrase therefore has phallic overtones. The word *woods* also suggests an area thickly populated with trees, while *industries* indicates that the case to be considered occurs during the industrial age. In the 1920s, Margaret Sanger pointed out that "today we are living in a world which is like a forest of trees too thickly planted [and] the rise in population, the multiplication of proletarian populations [is] a first result of mechanical industry" (*Pivot of Civilization* 268, 130). "Wood industries," then, reflects a popular belief that industry and overpopulation went hand-in-hand. By connecting "umbrella history" with "the wood industries," Joyce establishes the interrelatedness of contraception, overpopulation, and industry (business) at the outset of the trial.

The narrator (court reporter?) continues: "D'Oyly Owens holds (though Finn Magnusson of himself holds also) that so long as there is a joint deposit account in the two names a mutual obligation is posited" (*FW* 574.1–4). Thinly disguised in the terminology of the financial world used throughout the trial, this passage indicates that all traditional authorities have agreed that marriage or intercourse, the "joint deposit account," imposes a mutual obligation on the two spouses. It is not clear what that obligation is. Quoting St. Paul, *Casti Connubii* requires that in justice and charity "the husband render the debt to the wife, and the wife also in like manner to the husband" (quoted in Fremantle 237). Apparently the debt is the right of both the husband and the wife to indulge in unobstructed reproductive intercourse. For Marie Stopes and Margaret Sanger, the debt implied mutual orgasm without the fear of pregnancy (see Stopes 97, and Sanger, *The Pivot of Civilization* 214). The state, on the other hand (France, for example), argued that the debt or obligation included the responsibility to increase the population.

The next passage continues to set up the argument: "Owens cites Brerfuchs and Warren, a foreign firm, since disseized, registered as

Tangos Limited, for the sale of certain proprietary articles" (*FW* 574.5–7). "Brerfuchs and Warren" seems to be an Old Testament-like tradition, Genesis perhaps, or Vico's precivilized stage of existence, which insisted that men and women copulate and populate like rabbits (increase and multiply). The passage seems also to imply that only natural forces (like death at the hands of Brer Fox) are legitimate means of holding down the rabbit population. That ancient tradition has been taken over and modified by the Church, "Tangos Limited," which now has the power to "sell" (trade-off for her various blessings and indulgences) the right to copulate. The "proprietary articles," then, may be either sanctioned contraceptive practices (the "safe" period, permanent celibacy, etc.), the act of intercourse itself, or human lives (population).

The narrator next describes the action taken by the trustee of the complaining firm: "The action which was at the instance of the trustee of the heathen church emergency fund, suing by its trustee, a resigned civil servant, for the payment of tithes due was heard by Judge Doyle and also by a common jury. ... The defence alleged that payment had been made effective" (*FW* 574.6–14). This passage indicates that both the heathen church and its trustee, the "resigned civil servant" (i.e., nearly all institutions, religious and civil, outside the Church), are suing to obtain some of the power to control births, a power which the Church seems to have monopolized. Additionally, because it implies a competitive market in which the Church has established a monopoly on births, this passage recalls Margaret Sanger's closing statement at the anti-Comstock hearings in 1934. She insisted that "some church or other had acquired a monopoly on God's laws and Nature's, which, we were assured, were identical with patriotism and competitive procreation" (*My Fight For Birth Control* 351). But the defense in the Umbrella Case claims that payment "had been made effective." That is, the Church had not been withholding population.

In response,

> The fund trustee, one Jucundus Fecundus Xero Pecundus Copper-cheap, counterclaimed that payment was invalid having been tendered to creditor under cover of a crossed cheque, signed in the ordinary course, in the name of Wieldhelm, Hurls Cross, voucher copy provided, and drawn by the senior partner only by whom the lodgement of the species had been effected but in their joint names. (*FW* 574.12–17)

Here the trustee (now a businessman concerned about the increasingly low fertility rate of cheap laborers) counterclaims that, although the Church has not been withholding population, it has been making payments with a "crossed cheque." Furthermore, that cheque, a contraceptive practice approved ("crossed") by the Church in the name of God, can only be cashed by the Church itself, which claims to have charge of the survival of the entire species.

Here, Joyce surely had in mind the proprietary attitude of the Church toward marital intercourse crystallized in *Casti Connubii:* "How great is the dignity of chaste wedlock [the] foundation of domestic society and therefore of all human intercourse. [Through Christ, God has] entrusted all its discipline and care to His spouse the Church" (quoted in Fremantle 235). Sanger insisted that this encyclical represented a victory for the birth controllers because "it focalize[d] the center of the opposition to birth control in the Roman Catholic Church. (No one can any longer deny its aggressive enmity)" (*My Fight For Birth Control* 344).

Following the charges made by the fund trustee regarding the "crossed cheque" is a passage suggesting the persistent influence of Malthus. The reference to "the national misery" recalls Malthus's frequent use of that phrase in his "Essay on Population." Like virtually all birth controllers who followed Malthus, Sanger frequently argued that the national misery was caused by overpopulation. Mention of the national misery at this point in the Umbrella Case may also mark the point in the history of population control when the subject of the debate, the "stock," so to speak, went public. Once made public, the issue could no longer be controlled exclusively by the Church.

After an interlude where Coppercheap negotiates the cheque "for and on behalf of the fund of the thing"—that is, both to contribute to the population fund and to have fun—the cheque is transformed:

> Since then the cheque, a good washable pink, embossed D you D No 11 hundred and thirty 2, good for the figure and face, had been circulating in the country for over thirtynine years among holders of Pango stock, a rival concern, though not one demonetised farthing had ever spun or fluctuated across the counter in the semblance of hard coin or liquid cash. (*FW* 574.25–30)

The cheque has here become an artificial contraceptive. The gist of the passage is the following: since the dissemination of the Malthusian doctrine, the use of artificial checks on the population has become increasingly common; Anglicans (holders of Pango stock) have used them for thirty-nine years, apparently without suffering damnation. The contraceptive in question is undoubtedly a diaphragm because it is "washable" and "good for the figure and face."

It is interesting to note here how appropriate the word "cheque" is to Joyce's theme. Since Malthus published his "Essay on Population," the efficacy of various sorts of checks to the population have been debated. Famine, epidemics, war, celibacy, Onanism, "perverted" sex, artificial contraceptives have all been discussed in terms of their power to check the growth of the population. The identification of the "cheque" with currency also indicates the tendency (for which Marxists blamed Malthus) to reduce the populace to economic terms.

The French spelling of the word that Joyce uses in the Umbrella Case (which happens also to be the usual British and Irish spelling for a bank check) also suggests a French letter or condom. The "chequered staircase" leading to the Porter bedrooms (*FW* 560.9) mentioned earlier in the chapter reinforces the possibility that Joyce meant to suggest the French letter as well as other sorts of population checks by the various forms of "check" in the episode as a whole. Furthermore, the French have continued to keep their population under "control" since the 1870s—undoubtedly by artificial means—in spite of intense and long-standing campaigns by the Church and the state.

In addition to the abovementioned allusions of the word "cheque," there is a possible reference to one of the trials of Marie Stopes. In 1922 Stopes sued a Catholic physician, Dr. Halliday Sutherland, for libel. Sutherland had claimed that Stopes was prescribing devices that were both harmful and contrary to "decent instincts." The ensuing litigation lasted for two years, during which Sutherland's defense was financed by the Catholic community of Great Britain. The trial focused on Stopes's prescription of the "rubber check pessary" for her patients (Fryer 230–31). In *The Birth Controllers* Peter Fryer reports that the Roman Catholic campaign against Stopes was "unremitting." Furthermore, "in common with other birth control advocates, Marie Stopes suffered from a persistent rumour that each box of quinine and caco-butter suppositories contained a 'dud' " (Fryer 232). The "good washable pink" cheque "embossed D you D" that turns up in the Umbrella Case combines the qualities of the rubber check pessary and the alleged "duds" popularized in the accounts of Marie Stopes's trial.

The behavior of the judge and jury in the Umbrella Case seems also to parody the behavior of the judges and juries that tried Stopes,

Sanger, and their predecessor, Annie Besant, on various occasions. In the *Wake*, "The jury (a sour dozen of stout fellows all of whom were curiously named after doyles) naturally disagreed jointly and severally, and the belligerent judge, disagreeing with the allied jurors' disagreement, went outside his jurisfiction altogether and ordered a garnishee attachment to the neutral firm" (*FW* 574.30–35). In the Stopes libel case, finding that the words used by Sutherland were indeed defamatory, the jury awarded Stopes £100 in damages, but the Lord Chief Justice "interpreted the jury's contradictory findings to mean that Dr. Sutherland had won the action" (Fryer 231). In another hearing on contraceptives, Margaret Sanger records that to her chagrin, all of the members of the committee were Irish Roman Catholics ("curiously named after doyles"). And, at the conclusion of the Bradlaugh–Besant Trial, though the summation by Lord Chief Justice Cockburn was favorable to Bradlaugh and Besant, "the jury retired for an hour and thirty-five minutes discussing so fiercely that the noise could be heard outside the jury room" (Fryer 164). Still, the verdict was guilty.

The "junior partner" of the Breyfawkes firm, who appears in the Umbrella Case as "Barren," combines characteristics of her real-life sisters, the advocates of birth control. Barren turns out to be "an absolete turfwoman, originally from the proletarian class, with still a good title to her sexname of Ann Doyle, 2 Coppinger's Cottages, the Doyle's country" (*FW* 575.5–7). Campbell and Robinson identify Ann Doyle as "the Irish Catholic Wife" (332); however, the fact that Ann Doyle is also "Barren" makes that identification unlikely. During the 1920s and 1930s it was the common belief that Irish Catholic wives had the highest fertility rate of any group of women in the Western world. Indeed, that belief can be substantiated by statistics (see Kennedy).

Furthermore, although Ann Doyle is a "turfwoman," she is "absolete." Hence she is a type of woman both absent from and nonexistent on the "turf" of Ireland. I suggest that Ann Doyle is a feminist birth control advocate composed of fragments of the histories of the Irish-Englishwoman, Annie (Wood) Besant; the Irish-American, Margaret (Higgins) Sanger; and the Englishwoman, Dr. Marie Stopes. She may also be Joyce's vision of the future Irish wife, finally catching up with her more emancipated European and American counterparts.

It is obvious from the fact that he included Besant, Sanger, and Stopes in Jaun's sermon on the evil-pleasures of contraceptive sex that Joyce knew about the contributions these women had made to the history of population control. It is also clear from that sermon that Joyce thought of the birth controllers as a group. Since the *Wake* sees history (from one of its points-of-view) as a compost pile, it is likely that Joyce thought to compose, or compost, Ann Doyle from the leavings of three famous women birth controllers, all of whom were his contemporaries.

If he had investigated their lives and careers with even passing interest (biographies and autobiographical writings of all three women were available in the early 1930s), Joyce would have discovered a number of coincidences between their careers and his own. (As we know, Joyce delighted in coincidence.) At various times, the works of each of these women had been declared obscene and had involved them in years of litigation just as Joyce's works had done. On separate occasions in the 1920s and 1930s, Morris Ernst had acted as attorney for Joyce, Stopes, and Sanger. Marie Stopes's *Married Love* had been judged fit for Americans to read by the same Judge Woolsey who three years later would exonerate *Ulysses* (Maude 221).

It seems appropriate, then, that when Joyce was ready to "add woman in" (*FW* 575.7) to his "commonest of all cases arising out of umbrella history," he would add Annie Besant Marie Stopes Margaret Sanger Doyle. The Ann Doyle who appears in the Umbrella Case is there, at least initially, to defend the use of contraceptives. Indeed, Ann Doyle, who is "absolete" and therefore probably an exile, is somewhat Shemlike, for she "protested cheerfully on the stand in a long jurymiad" (*FW* 575.8–9).

The subject of Ann Doyle's "jurymiad" is "corset checks" which she is accused of having supplied in response to "brusk demands." The terms of her checks are "nine months from date without issue" (*FW* 575.10–12). All three of the birth controllers defended themselves and the right of women to know about female contraceptives because they perceived a great demand in the community. Each of them might be said to have delivered "jurymiads" in defense of "corset checks." Annie Besant's "lengthy address" to the jury at the Bradlaugh–Besant trial, for example, was described in the press as a "tour de force" (Fryer 162). The judge who heard Marie Stopes's appeal of a guilty verdict in a libel case called her argument "forcible and intelligent." He did not reverse the decision, however (Maude 212).

Sanger's campaign for birth control involved her in numerous schemes to smuggle diaphragms into the United States, the first attempt being made when she returned to the United States after a self-imposed exile. Sanger "got hold of some diaphragms and experimented with flattening and hiding them under her girdle" (corset?) (Gray 63). In 1935 she financed the defense in the widely reported case of "The United States versus One Package of Japanese Pessaries." Morris Ernst pleaded and won the case for the pessaries (Gray 357–65).

The "jurymiad" which Ann Doyle delivers in the Umbrella Case recounts how Ann herself

> unbottled in corrubberation on a current account of how she had been made for services rendered the payee-drawee of unwashable blank assignations, sometimes pinkwilliams (laughter) but more often of the *crème-de-citron, vair email paoncoque* or marshmallow series, which she, as bearer, used to endorse, adhesively, to her various payers-drawers. (*FW* 575.13–18)

Each of the three birth controllers insisted that since it is the woman who is the "bearer," it must be the woman who decides when and how often to bear. Joyce appears to be responding to that emphasis in the passage just quoted.

The contraceptive devices and potions suggested in the passage, materials that Ann both gives to and receives from her payers-drawers, are described in detail in Margaret Sanger's pamphlet *Family Limitation*, a publication she was required to defend in court. The 1915 version of the pamphlet includes "Methods for Husbands" and "Methods for Wives." In order of desirability, the diaphragm ranks first for wives; however, "a woman was advised to keep a supply of condoms on hand and try to slip one onto the penis of an amorous husband ["endorse, adhesively"?] when he was too drunk to do it himself" (Gray 102). Before diaphragms became legal in the United States (as a result of the case won by Ernst), Sanger had commissioned an Italian coal-man to smuggle Dutch pessaries into the country in liquor bottles (Gray 200–201). Knowing this, it is tempting to read "unbottled in corrubberation" as a reference to Sanger's Dutch-Italian connection.

In the final portion of the Umbrella Case, Ann Doyle proposes to share with the Catholic Church, now represented by "Monsignore Pepigi," her newly realized power over population. She makes her offer contingent on Pepigi's agreement to allow birth control "under the new style of Will Breakfast and Sparrem" (*FW* 575.29–30). I understand the new style to involve breaking a fast sparingly as well as sparing unwanted children. Ann Doyle is apparently requesting a compromise much like that offered by the Lambeth Conference of 1930.

Ann Doyle's "prepopsal" (presumptuous, preposterous proposal to preempt the power of the pope?) was "ruled out on appeal by Judge Jeremy Doyler, who ... handed down to the jury of the Liffey that, as a matter of tact, the woman they gave as free was born into contractual incapacity (the Calif of Man v the Eaudelusk Company) when, how and

where mamy's mancipium act did not apply" (*FW* 575.31–576.4).
Clearly the Church refuses to recognize women's right to control the
population. Besides echoing *Casti Connubii*, this passage recalls the sce-
narios at most of the trials where birth control was the issue. It suggests,
too, the 1929 Irish Censorship Bill.

The Umbrella Case closes on a note of apparent finality. The
Church, or some power in authority over women, will retain the right to
control the population. At the conclusion of the trial Ann is more clearly
identifiable as the Irish wife, or Ireland itself. Irish wives are among the
few women who have submitted to the laws of the Church regarding
birth control (though, according to Kevin R. O'Reilly, there are definite
signs that Irish women are currently taking charge of their reproductive
lives). However, we do not learn whether Ann Doyle submits to the decision of Judge Doyler. Once a woman knows the power of a "corset
check," it is not likely that she will relinquish that power to any one. If
need be, she will simply find another judge, as Margaret Sanger did, a
judge who is not an Irish Catholic. Finally, the Umbrella Trial seems to
do precisely what the birth control movement of the 1920s and 1930s
did: it isolated "as a Roman Catholic specialty, the opposition to the use
of contraceptives" (Fryer). By the end of the 1930s, the Catholic Church
was the only international power officially and unequivocally opposed to
birth control. Even so, Ireland is one of the few countries of the Western
world that seems to have submitted to that authority.

Neither Judge Doyle nor Ann Doyle has the last word in the *Wake*.
As we know, there is no last word. ALP, the life force, makes individual
acts of contraception seem irrelevant as she goes on controlling (or un-
controlling) the population in spite of famine, war, and diaphragms. Yet
the *Wake* reveals the influence and significance of the campaign for birth
control in important ways. The *Wake* is about a family, one that has been
planned to be just the right size. The very structure of the family in the
Wake—father, mother, two boys, and a girl—matches what had come to
be the desirable middle-class family in the second decade of this century.

As Fryer points out, by the time the Malthusian League resumed
its campaign after the First World War (with Arnold Bennett and H. G.
Wells as vice-presidents), "the family of four or five [children] had become the family of two or three" (240). By the end of the 1930s, "Birth
Control" had given way to "Family Planning" or "Planned Parenthood,"
and conscious, careful begetting was being stressed by the middle and
upper classes. Because parents had fewer children, those children were
more closely scrutinized and, in many ways, under more pressure to be
successful. Children were expected to prove the success of their parents

as parents. Conversely, the children were more likely to call into account the performance of parents who now had relatively few children to attend to. Similarly, in the *Wake,* as Bernard Benstock points out, "the three children expand to become all-inclusive [and furthermore] the five characters besetting H. C. E. are themselves the five members of the Earwicker family" (*Joyce-Again's Wake* 26). Even in its structures, then, the *Wake* is very much involved in the discourse on population control which helped form it. Once birth control became respectable, once women asserted their right to bear or not bear children, family politics were called up for questioning. The *Wake* reproduces the trial in progress.

Conclusion

Joyce's interest in population problems came naturally to him. In Ireland, the concern with demographics dates back at least as far as the Great Famine, when it seemed as though all of Ireland would be absorbed by America. From that time, to leave the country became at once the most natural and the most unnatural thing to do. Those who stayed behind adapted to conflicting economic and religious pressures by creating some of the most bizarre and contradictory fertility patterns in the Western world. From the mid-nineteenth century until the 1980s, Ireland has recorded the highest rates of permanent male celibacy and the greatest marital fertility rates of any Western nation. During the same period, emigration rates have continued to significantly exceed those of other Western countries. All of these demographic "aberrations" have been endlessly discussed in Ireland with a view toward curing or excusing them.

Outside of Ireland, especially in interwar Europe, Joyce was to discover that population control was not an exclusively Irish fixation, but was universally debated, imposed, and resisted. He was able to examine the demographic patterns of a larger world and to discover how his microscopic world matched up, just as he was able to examine universal moral and artistic values in light of Irish mores. Two of the major contenders in the debate about population control in the Western world at large were the same as the litigants in the trial at home: the Church and Malthus. Therefore, Joyce features their doctrines, in all of their modifications, in his works.

Commenting (in a note) on Jaun's sermon in the *Wake,* Adaline Glasheen nicely ties together the apparently diverse elements of population control in Joyce's works, elements that I have highlighted in this study:

101

> Like "The Waste Land," *Ulysses* and *Finnegans Wake* are predicated
> on the ancient proposition: physical fertility and spiritual fertility
> are interchangeable counters in the literary game. Can these count-
> ers bring esthetic response from citizens of a world committed to
> zero population growth? There is no use saying Joyce didn't know
> what overpopulation means. The Irish did know and before the rest
> of western Europe. "In 1845 the population had swelled to
> 8,295,061, the greater part of whom depended on the potato." (*lxi*)

In these comments, Glasheen demonstrates that she recognizes the links
in Joyce's works between specifically Irish population problems—
heightened by the Famine—and the subject matter and techniques of
those works. Furthermore, she admits into her discussion "the ancient
proposition," which, as Joyce discovered, was being challenged in the
Western world as a whole. Finally, Glasheen suggests that Joyce saw a
profound (real) relationship between physical and artistic/spiritual
fertility.

Joyce's tendency to see the world in terms of its vital statistics might
be summed up in the conundrum "Is life worth living?" which appears
in several forms in the *Wake*. Patrick McCarthy points out that the two
forms "Was liffe worth leaving?" (*FW* 230.25) and "Is love worse living?"
(269.n.1) ultimately incorporate "not only life but exile from Dublin and
the Liffey, death, and love" (*Riddles* 18–19). In this unanswerable riddle
embedded in his final work, Joyce still exhibits the typically Irish conflict
about emigrating. He also asks the questions raised by the birth controllers and their opponents: Is life, all life, as much life as possible, worth
leaving behind for posterity? What is the relationship between loving
and living? Between loving and giving life?

McCarthy observes that an early passage in the *Wake* (where Earwicker muses about the hen) "suggests that it is the cyclic, repetitive nature of life—made possible by Anna Livia Plurabelle ... that makes life
worth living" in spite of war, birth control, or religion (*Riddles* 19): "She
is livving in our midst of debt and laffing through all plores for us (her
birth is uncontrollable). ... Gricks may rise and Troysirs fall (there being
two sights for ever a picture) for in the byways of high improvidence
that's what makes lifework leaving and the world's a cell for citters to cit
in." (*FW* 11.32–12.2)

Assuming that it is necessary to come to a conclusion about the attitude toward population control in Joyce's works (the structure of the
Wake indicates that it is neither necessary nor possible), that conclusion
would have to be summed up in the parenthetical description of ALP
given above. "Her birth is uncontrollable."

Works Cited

Averill, Deborah M. *The Irish Short Story From George Moore to Frank O'Connor.* Washington, D.C.: Univ. Press of America, 1982.

Benjamin, Walter. "Edward Fuchs, Collector and Historian." In *One Way Street and Other Writings.* London: New Left Books, 1979.

Benstock, Bernard. *James Joyce: The Undiscover'd Country.* Dublin: Gill & Macmillan, 1977.

———. *Joyce-Again's Wake.* Seattle: Univ. of Washington Press, 1965.

Benstock, Shari. "Sexuality and Survival in *Finnegans Wake.*" In *The Seventh of Joyce,* edited by Bernard Benstock. Bloomington: Indiana Univ. Press, 1982.

"Birth Control Movement." *The New Catholic Encyclopedia.* New York: McGraw-Hill, 1967.

Bowen, Zack. "Joyce's Prophylactic Paralysis: Exposure in *Dubliners.*" *James Joyce Quarterly* 19 (Spring 1982): 257–73.

Brown, Richard. *James Joyce and Sexuality.* London: Cambridge Univ. Press, 1985.

Cahalan, James M. *Great Hatred, Little Room: The Irish Historical Novel.* Syracuse: Syracuse Univ. Press, 1983.

Campbell, Joseph, and Henry Morton Robinson. *A Skeleton Key to "Finnegans Wake."* New York: Penguin, 1986.

Carens, James F. "Some Points on Poyntz and Related Matters." *James Joyce Quarterly* 16 (Spring 1979): 344–46.

Carr-Saunders, Alexander Morris. *The Population Problem: A Study in Human Evolution.* Oxford: Clarendon Press, 1922.

Chandrasekhar, S. *"A Dirty Filthy Book": The Writings of Charles Knowlton and Annie Besant on Reproductive Physiology and Birth Control and an Account of the Bradlaugh–Besant Trial.* Berkeley and Los Angeles: Univ. of California Press, 1981.

Chase, Allan. *The Legacy of Malthus: The Social Costs of the New Scientific Racism.* New York: Knopf, 1977.

Cixous, Helene. *The Exile of James Joyce*. Translated by Sally A. J. Purcell. London: John Calder, 1976.

Cousens, S. H. "Population Trends in Ireland at the Beginning of the Twentieth Century." *Irish Geography* 5, no. 5 (1968): 387–401.

Daryl, Phillippe. *Ireland's Disease*. London: Routledge, 1888.

Davitt, Michael. *The Fall of Feudalism in Ireland*. London: Harper & Brothers, 1904.

Dolch, Martin. "Eveline." In *James Joyce's "Dubliners": A Critical Handbook*, edited by James R. Baker and Thomas F. Staley. Belmont, Calif.: Wadsworth, 1969.

Dyer, Colin. *Population and Society in Twentieth Century France*. New York: Holmes & Meier, 1978.

The Egoist (1914).

Ellis, Havelock. *Studies in the Psychology of Sex*. Vol. 2. New York: Random House, 1936.

Ellman, Richard. *The Consciousness of Joyce*. New York: Oxford Univ. Press, 1977.

———. *James Joyce*. Oxford: Oxford Univ. Press, 1982.

Epstein, Edmund. "James Augustine Aloysius Joyce." In *A Companion to Joyce Studies*, edited by Zack Bowen and James F. Carens. Westport, Conn.: Greenwood Press, 1984.

Ervine, St. John G. "Francis Place." Fabian Tract no. 165. London: The Fabian Society, 1919.

"Famine." *Encyclopaedia Britannica*, 14th ed.

Flanagan, Thomas. *The Irish Novelists: 1800–1850*. New York: Columbia Univ. Press, 1958.

Foucault, Michel. *The History of Sexuality: Volume 1: An Introduction*. New York: Random House, 1980.

———. "What Is An Author?" In *Textual Strategies: Perspectives in Post-Structural Criticism*, edited by Josué V. Harai. Ithaca: Cornell Univ. Press, 1979.

Fremantle, Anne, ed. *The Papal Encyclicals*. New York: New American Library, 1963.

Fryer, Peter. *The Birth Controllers*. New York: Stein & Day, 1965.

Fussell, Paul. *The Great War and Modern Memory*. Oxford: Oxford Univ. Press, 1975.

Gallagher, Thomas. *Paddy's Lament: Ireland 1846–1847: Prelude to Hatred*. New York: Harcourt, 1982.

Geary, R. C. "Present Day and Future Emigration from Ireland in Historical Perspective." Paper presented to seminar in the Department of Economic and Social History, The Queen's University, Belfast, 3 May 1968.

Glasheen, Adaline. *Third Census of "Finnegans Wake."* Berkeley and Los Angeles: Univ. of California Press, 1977.

Glass, David Victor. *Population Policies and Movements in Europe*. Oxford: Clarendon Press, 1940.

Gordon, John. *"Finnegans Wake": A Plot Summary*. Syracuse: Syracuse Univ. Press, 1986.

Gray, Madeline. *Margaret Sanger.* New York: Richard Marek Publishers, 1979.

Greenblatt, Stephen. *Renaissance Self-Fashioning from More to Shakespeare.* Chicago: Univ. of Chicago Press, 1980.

Gwynn, Stephen. *Today and Tomorrow in Ireland: Essays on Irish Subjects.* Dublin: Hodges, Figgis, 1903.

Herr, Cheryl. *Joyce's Anatomy of Culture.* Urbana: Univ. of Illinois Press, 1986.

"Household Hints." *Irish Homestead,* 13 August 1904, 674.

"Ireland." *London Times,* 30 May 1904, 10.

Joyce, Stanislaus. *My Brother's Keeper.* New York: Viking, 1958.

Kavanagh, Patrick. "The Great Hunger." In *The Faber Book of Contemporary Irish Poetry,* edited by Paul Muldoon. London: Faber & Faber, 1986.

Kennedy, Robert E. *The Irish: Emigration, Marriage, and Fertility.* Berkeley and Los Angeles: Univ. of California, 1973.

Keynes, R. "Malthus and Biological Equilibria." In *Malthus Past and Present,* edited by J. Dupaquier. London: Academy Press, 1983.

Kiberd, Declan. "The Perils of Nostalgia: A Critique of the Revival." In *Literature and the Changing Ireland,* edited by Peter Connolly. Totowa, N.J.: Barnes & Noble, 1982.

"The Labour Problem." *Irish Homestead,* 13 August 1904, 663.

Lawless, Emily. *The Story of Ireland.* New York: G. P. Putnam, 1888.

Lecky, William Edward Hartpole. *The History of European Morals.* Vol. 2. London: Longmans, Green, 1869.

McCarthy, Patrick A. *The Riddles of "Finnegans Wake."* London: Associated Univ. Press, 1980.

———. "Structures and Meanings of *Finnegans Wake.*" In *A Companion to Joyce Studies,* edited by Zack Bowen and James F. Carens. Westport, Conn.: Greenwood Press, 1984.

McCartny, Donal. "From Parnell to Pearse (1891–1921)." In *The Course of Irish History,* edited by T. W. Moody and F. X. Martin. Cork, Ireland: Mercier Press, 1987.

Magalaner, Marvin, and Richard M. Kain. "*Dubliners* and the Short Story." In *James Joyce's "Dubliners": A Critical Handbook,* edited by James R. Baker and Thomas F. Staley. Belmont, Calif.: Wadsworth, 1969.

Malthus, Thomas Robert. *On Population.* Edited by Gertrude Himmelfarb. New York: Modern Library, 1960.

Manganiello, Dominic. *Joyce's Politics.* London: Routledge & Kegan Paul, 1980.

Maude, Aylmer. *Marie Stopes: Her Work and Play.* New York: G. P. Putnam, 1933.

Moore, George. *The Untilled Field.* London: T. Fisher Unwin, 1903.

Noonan, John T. "Contraception." In *The Encyclopedia of Bioethics,* edited by Warren T. Reich. New York: Free Press, 1978.

———. *Contraception: A History of Its Treatment by the Catholic Theologians and Canonists.* Cambridge, Mass.: Harvard Univ. Press, 1966.

Norris, Margot. *The Decentered Universe of "Finnegans Wake."* Baltimore: Johns Hopkins Univ. Press, 1976.

O'Brien, John A., ed. *The Vanishing Irish: The Enigma of the Modern World.* New York: McGraw-Hill, 1953.

O'Connor, Ulick. *Celtic Dawn: A Portrait of the Irish Literary Renaissance.* London: Black Swan, 1985.

O'Reilly, Kevin R. "Contraception, Ideology and Policy Formation: Cohort Change in Dublin, Ireland." In *Culture and Reproduction,* edited by W. Penn Handwerker. Boulder, Colo.: Westview Press, 1986.

O'Rourke, John. *The History of the Great Irish Famine of 1847.* Dublin: McGlashan & Gill, 1875.

Paul-Dubois, L. *Contemporary Ireland.* Dublin: Maunsel, 1908.

Plunkett, Horace. *Ireland in the New Century.* London: John Murray, 1904.

"Population Ethics: Basic Elements." In *The Encyclopedia of Bioethics,* edited by Warren T. Reich. New York: Free Press, 1978.

Ross, Eric B. "Potatoes, Population, and the Irish Famine: The Political Economy of Demographic Change." In *Culture and Reproduction,* edited by W. Penn Handwerker. Boulder, Colo.: Westview Press, 1986.

Sanger, Margaret. *My Fight for Birth Control.* New York: Farrar & Rinehart, 1931.

———. *The New Motherhood.* London: Jonathan Cape, 1922.

———. *The Pivot of Civilization.* New York: Brentano's, 1922.

Scott, Bonnie Kime. *James Joyce.* Brighton, England: Harvester Press, 1987.

———. *Joyce and Feminism.* Bloomington: Indiana Univ. Press, 1984.

Shaw, George Bernard. Preface to *Getting Married.* In *Plays.* Vol. 12. New York: Wm. H. Wise & Co., 1930.

Sheridan, John Desmond. *James Clarence Mangan.* Dublin: Talbot Press, 1937.

Solomon, Margaret. "The Porters: A Square Performance of Three Tiers in the Round/Book III, chapter iv." In *A Conceptual Guide to "Finnegans Wake,"* edited by Michael H. Begnal and Fritz Senn. University Park: Pennsylvania State Univ. Press, 1974.

Soloway, Richard Allen. *Birth Control and the Population Question in England 1877–1930.* Chapel Hill: Univ. of North Carolina Press, 1982.

Stopes, Marie Carmichael. *Married Love.* New York: Truth Publishing Company, 1918.

Sulloway, Alvah W. *Birth Control and Catholic Doctrine.* Boston: Beacon Press, 1959.

"The Untilled Field." *Dublin Daily Express,* September 3, 1903, 7.

Walzl, Florence. *"Dubliners."* In *A Companion to Joyce Studies,* edited by Zack Bowen and James F. Carens. Westport, Conn.: Greenwood Press, 1984.

Webb, Sidney. "The Decline in the Birth-Rate." Fabian Tract no. 131. London: The Fabian Society, 1907.

Woodham-Smith, Cecil. *The Great Hunger: Ireland 1845–1849.* New York: Harper & Row, 1962.

Yeats, W. B. *The Countess Cathleen.* In *The Collected Plays of W. B. Yeats.* New York: Macmillan, 1952.

Index

"Aeolus," 70
"After the Race," 44
American Wake, 28–29
anemia metaphor, of Ireland's condition,
    14, 15, 22, 23, 24, 31–32, 37, 39, 76
Anglican church, and birth control, 25,
    80. *See also* Lambeth Conference
Anglo-Irish guerrilla war, 54
Anti-Emigration Society, 31, 37
Archer, William, 13
"Aristotle on Education," 23
Aristotle on reproduction, 67
Augustine, *Marriage and Concupiscence*,
    63
author-function, 6–7
Averill, Deborah M., 34, 41

bachelors, in Joyce's works, 2, 9. *See also*
    celibacy
Benstock, Bernard, 24, 90, 99
Besant, Annie, 79–80, 81, 83, 85, 95;
    trial of, 25, 59, 60, 65, 73, 80, 90, 95,
    96
birth control: and Anglican church, 25,
    80; in *Finnegans Wake*, 78, 80; Joyce's
    attitude toward, 67–68, 72–74; in
    "Oxen of the Sun," 68–74; as
    population control, 56, 78, 80, 86, 95,
    99; and Roman Catholic church, 4, 9,
    25, 27, 62–63, 67, 68–69, 73, 80, 86,

93, 98; in *Ulysses*, 62. *See also* birth
    control movement; contraceptives
birth control movement, 3, 25–28, 54,
    58–60, 75, 77, 80–83, 86, 88, 89–
    99; as family planning, 28, 77, 98–
    99; pioneers of, 79–80; and
    population control, 1, 3, 22, 55, 80,
    86. *See also* Besant, Annie; birth
    control; population control; Sanger,
    Margaret; Stopes, Dr. Marie
Blunden, Edmund, *Undertones of War*,
    57–58
"Boarding House, The," 9
Bowen, Zack, 61
Bradlaugh, Charles, 25, 59, 60, 65, 73,
    80, 95, 96
Brilliant Career, A, 13
Brown, Richard, 25, 26, 50, 55, 59, 62,
    71, 86
Byrne, John Francis, 21

Carens, James F., 62
Carr-Saunders, Alexander Morris, *The
    Population Problem: A Study in Human
    Evolution*, 77
Casti Connubii, 25, 80, 87, 89, 91, 93, 98
Catholic church. *See* Roman Catholic
    church
celibacy, 1, 21, 67; permanent male, 6, 8–
    9, 101

107